BUSINESS AS USUAL

Business as Usual

EDMUNDO WERNA

Avebury

Aldershot · Brookfield USA · Hong Kong · Singapore · Sydney

Published by
Avebury
Ashgate Publishing Ltd
Gower House
Croft Road
Aldershot
Hants GU11 3HR
England

Ashgate Publishing Company
Old Post Road
Brookfield
Vermont 05036
USA

British Library Cataloguing in Publication Data

Werna, Edmundo
  Business as usual
  1. Housing development - Developing countries 2. Construction
  industry - Appropriate technology - Developing countries
  3. Poor - Housing - Developing countries
  I. Title
  363.5 '1' 091724

  ISBN 1 85972 354 3

Library of Congress Catalog Card Number: 96-84016

Printed and bound in Great Britain by Ipswich Book Co. Ltd., Ipswich, Suffolk

Contents

Tables

Acknowledgements

The contributions to this book are not restricted to the people who supported my work during the process of research and writing up. Without the support of many others in previous periods, I would not have even started this project. It is not possible here to mention everyone. They all have my deepest gratitude, specially Miloquinha Werna Salvo, who always gave great support for my academic activities (among many other things), to whom I dedicate this book. I would also like to pay homage to my grandfather, Ernesto Frederico Werna, and to my father, Augusto Werna, who inspired me with their histories.

Interest in the theme of this book originated from my early experience in urban development assignments, which started in the late 1970s, when I was still doing my graduate studies. In this regard, I thank my first boss, Maria Lucia Malard, who gave me her vital support especially (but not only) in the early stages of my career.

I carried out the research project which provided the basis for this book at the Development Planning Unit (DPU), University College London. From the DPU I thank Ronaldo Ramirez for supervision, and Patrick Wakely for his comments and managerial backing. Still on the academic side, I thank Regina Celia Claro, Michael Edwards, Chris Gerry, Paulo Haddad, Ramin Keyvani, Sunil Kumar, Ann Varley and Jill Wells who read previous versions of the manuscript and gave me their comments - and, equally important, gave me their friendly support. I also thank all those who supported the field work, especially the master builder Antonio Luis, who was a great source of inspiration, and Luis Felipe Calvo. In the post-manuscript stage of the book (i.e. revision and preparation for printing), I thank Regina Celia Claro and Leandro Coelho for their help. Finally, I thank my current research partners, especially Trudy Harpham, Alex Abiko and Ilona Blue. Although our current work has not been directly related to this book, their support in the present stage of my career has given me energy and motivation to finish this extensive project.

On the financial side, I thank the following institutions for their support during different periods: British Council, Deans Scholarship Scheme of the University College London, Department of Civil Construction Engineering of the University of São Paulo, CAPES and CNPq.

Introduction

Interest in the theme of this book originated from the author's professional experience in low-income settlements in developing countries, from the late-1970s to the 1990s. It was evident that the urban poor did not have access to most public housing schemes and to finished housing built by large-scale private contractors. They had to seek alternative ways to build gradually, according to what they could afford. This situation has led many authors to praise the 'self-help' housing process - i.e. housing built by the owner alone or with the help of relatives and/or friends. However, enthusiasm with this process has often led to gross generalisations regarding what has actually taken place in low-income settlements. The local individuals or groups frequently seen working in low-income housing construction are often paid contractors. A vast number of poor people do not have the expertise and also the time to carry out most stages of the building process. In addition, they seldom have relatives or friends with both the know-how and the availability to carry out all these stages. As a result, they have resorted to small-scale private contractors to carry out at least the most significant parts of the building process - and often the entire process.

Therefore, the low-income settlements and their process of construction - which have frequently been regarded as something entirely different and separate from the 'formal' parts of the cities - are also permeated by market relations. It is *business as usual* in low-income settlements.

Such observations were supported by a number of authors who highlighted similar occurrences in different settlements in developing countries (e.g. Bienefeld, 1979; Burgess, 1992; IBAM, 1982, 1986; Inyang, 1987; Johnstone, 1978, 1984; Maricato, 1987; Mautner, 1987, 1989, 1991; Ozuekren, 1989; PADCO/USAID, 1985; Phillip, 1987; Rakodi, 1989; Rasmussen, 1990; Taschner and Mautner, 1982; Tuffs, 1987; Wycliffe, 1987). Also, there has been a growing interest of international organizations and a number of authors in formulating policies to increase the participation of small-scale builders in the production of low-cost urban housing.

During the period of observation of the activities of the small-scale builders, attention was drawn to the fact that they were the least supported and least equipped agents within the construction industry. Yet, these builders played a pivotal role in

1

low-cost housing production. The awareness about this situation prompted an inquiry as to *why they are capable of producing low-cost housing, even under unfavourable conditions.*

During this period of observation, attention was also drawn to the fact that the builders did not constitute a static group. There were always new builders setting up businesses in low-income settlements, and others moving elsewhere. The awareness of the existence of such factors prompted an inquiry as to the dynamics of change regarding these builders - *where do they come from, where are they going to, what are the factors related to their movements.*

Considering that the builders worked under adverse conditions (e.g. badly-equipped, using elementary technology), support for them seemed to be favourable. This inference was substantiated by the growing body of literature already mentioned, which led to the formulation of policies to strengthen the position of these builders. However, it was not clear how the insertion of exogenous elements such as new technology, credit and training would affect the activities of the builders in low-cost housing production. Considering that they had characteristics which enabled them to build low-cost housing, it was necessary to assess how the new elements would affect such characteristics, and, consequently, affect the supply of low-cost housing.

In summary, the observation of the activities of small-scale builders in low-income settlements and the main focus of the literature related to the subject motivated an inquiry as to the factors which enable these builders to carry out their activities, as to their dynamics of change, and as to the effect of exogenous support in their activities.

The specific investigation for this book began by analysing the literature on the small-scale production of low-cost housing in developing countries in detail to see how the above issues had been approached. This analysis highlighted a set of attributes which make small-scale contractors beneficial to the supply of low-cost housing. However, the literature does not explain why the producers have such attributes, nor how they apply to the specific characteristics of low-cost housing.

The analysis of the prevailing knowledge of the subject also reveals that there is a dilemma regarding the provision of exogenous support to the builders, and their participation in low-cost housing production. This provision opens up the possibility for the builders to capitalize. This, in turn, may drive them away from low-cost housing production.

Based on the above issues, this book addresses the following questions:

> *Why are small-scale builders capable of producing low-cost housing in developing countries?*

> *What are the constraints on capitalization experienced by small-scale builders, and how does their removal affect the participation of the builders in the provision of low-cost housing?*

After examining the theoretical approaches to small-scale production of low-cost housing in developing countries, the petty-commodity production approach was chosen to analyze the above questions. Small-scale builders are characterized as non-capitalist producers, and the petty-commodity production approach is used to develop

2

this concept and provide the basis for the construction of the theoretical framework of the book. This framework, in turn, gives origin to two sets of tentative answers to the above questions.

The first set concerns the characteristics of small-scale builders, and suggests that these are related to the character of the demand for low-cost housing in developing countries. For the purpose of this book, this demand is characterized as being diversified, discontinuous, small-scale and capable only of atomized disbursements. The builders are able to meet it by employing a process of production which has a degree of flexibility together with prices for services which satisfy its specific characteristics.

The second set concerns the support of small-scale builders and the provision of low-cost housing. It suggests that the implementation of policies of provision of credit, equipment and managerial and labour force capacity to the builders will lead them towards capitalist production, which, in turn, will drive them away from low-cost housing production. The fact that small-scale builders work in low-income settlements does not mean that they will necessarily do voluntary work to help the poor. Regardless of who their clients are, it is *business as usual* for professional builders. Thus, if they are able to cater for more lucrative activities outside low-income settlements, they will leave these settlements.

Having defined its main questions and their tentative answers, the book presents conceptual and empirical material to substantiate the answers. The latter includes primary data from Brazil, and references to other developing countries based on the work of a number of authors. The findings of this analysis confirm the aforementioned answers, showing that, if support is given to builders, they move from a stage of non-capitalist (petty-commodity) production, when they build low-cost housing, towards a stage of capitalist production. However, during this process, they lose the characteristics which enabled them to supply low-cost housing in the first place.

The assertion that the provision of support opens up possibilities for capitalization for small-scale builders does not mean that small-scale low-cost housing production will disappear. The lacunae left empty by the builders who moved may be filled by newcomers. However, *other things being equal, the support for builders will not increase their participation in low-cost housing production.* This reasoning could lead one to infer that the best solution would be to leave builders without support, i.e. as backward as possible. However, this is not the proposal made here.

The book entails a *ceteris paribus* condition, and asserts that the support given to small-scale builders may fortify the building industry as a whole, through improvements in equipment, credit, managerial and labour force capacity, and the like. However, if it bolsters the current structure of capitalist production within the industry, it will not ameliorate automatically the provision of low-cost housing.

However, rather than preventing small-scale builders from capitalizing, different routes could be taken. First, if the demand for low-cost housing were fostered, the poor could have access to a wider range of agents within the building industry. Also, ways could be found to support the development of builders to enable them to implement small-scale but high-technology flexible units of production rather than the current capitalist large-scale fordist-type ones (Werna, 1994). Another possibility would be to focus on ways through which the current capitalist producers could reach the poor. It is suggested here that these routes open up some avenues for future research.

The transformation of non-capitalist (petty-commodity) units of production into capitalist ones is not seen in this book as the only viable progression for a builder. For instance, according to the circumstances, it is also possible that a capitalist unit goes back to a petty-commodity production stage, or that a petty-commodity producer stagnates or becomes proletarian rather than capitalize. However, the aim here is not to explore the full range of possibilities, but to analyze the specific process of capitalization of builders.

When referring to small-scale production, different authors use different units of analysis, such as the unit of production (i.e. the firm, the enterprise), the individual, or the household. This book focuses on the *unit of production*. In order to alleviate the monotony of using the same term throughout the whole text, the terms *builder*, *contractor* and *producer* also will be used, as synonyms for unit of production. It is important to understand that this builder/contractor/producer is the unit of production, even if working alone, because there is a direct producer-consumer relationship between him and the client. This social actor is different from a labourer, who has a relation of production *within* the unit a production, and does not entail a relation between producer and client.

The book briefly described above is here presented by means of six chapters.

Chapter 1 analyzes the literature and its different theoretical approaches to small-scale production of low-cost housing in developing countries. Special attention is given to the factors which enable small-scale builders to produce low-cost housing, to the process of development of builders, and to the effects of this process on their activities in low-income settlements. The problems of each approach are pointed out, and it is shown that the initial queries of the book have not been properly addressed in the literature. Also, it is shown that one of the approaches, petty-commodity production, provides a basis for the development of a theoretical framework for the book.

Chapter 2 presents the theoretical core of the book. The problems which were highlighted in the previous chapter are here elaborated with the help of the petty-commodity production approach.

Chapter 3 examines the factors which enable small-scale builders to produce low-cost housing. The analysis concentrates on prices and flexibility of production.

Chapters 4 and 5 are concerned with factors which constrain the growth of small-scale builders, and the effect of their removal on the way builders produce low-cost housing. Four factors are analyzed: blocked access to equipment, to labour capacity, to managerial capacity and to credit.

Finally, Chapter 6 puts together the main points of the previous chapters, identifies their policy implications and suggests avenues for future research.

1 Theoretical approaches

The theoretical approaches to small-scale production of low-cost housing in developing countries can be divided into five: liberal neo-classical, appropriate technology, modes of production, transfer of surplus and petty-commodity production. The analysis of each approach prioritizes the conceptualization of small-scale producers, the factors which enable them to or constrain them from producing low-cost housing, policies proposed to eliminate constraints, and the process of development of these producers.

Liberal neo-classical

This section starts by tracing the origins of the liberal neo-classical approach in the literature on small-scale urban production in general. Next, it narrows the focus to the specific field of low-cost housing production.

The term liberal neo-classical was used by Moser to define an approach within the literature on small-scale urban production which depicts the urban economy divided into two separate sectors, the small-scale producers as evolutionary and independent from large-scale ones, and which encourages cooperation between these two types of producers as being beneficial to both (Moser, 1984). For the purpose of this book, the term liberal neo-classical refers exclusively to this body of argument.

The dualist view of the urban economy in developing countries has generated different concepts, such as a bazaar-type and a firm centred economy, enumerated and non-enumerated sector, formal and informal sector, among others. However, as Schmitz shows, despite the different terms, these authors broadly refer to the same group of producers or units of production: small-scale, on the one side, and large-scale, on the other (Schmitz, 1982). Amongst all the different pairs of concepts, the formal-informal sector is the most used in the literature on small-scale production in general as well as in housing in particular. The widespread use of the concept calls for a more elaborate analysis.

The term informal sector was introduced by Hart based on research in Ghana (Hart, 1971). He made a distinction between a 'formal' sector - units of production with waged workers recruited on a permanent and regular basis - and an 'informal' one - an unorganised sector of self-employment. After Hart, other definitions for the in/formal sectors have been put forward, such as a separation within the labour market rather than between units of production (Mazundar, 1975), or a distinction based on the kind of relationship that each sector has vis-a-vis the state - the formal sector consists of private enterprises recognized, supported and regulated by the state, plus the public enterprises, while the informal sector consists of private enterprises with an opposite relation vis-a-vis the state (Weeks, 1973). The definition given by the mission of the International Labour Office to Kenya is the most widely used, and it refers explicitly to small-scale producers (ILO, 1972). This definition is based on the characteristics of the units of production: small-scale operations, facility of entry, reliance on indigenous resources, family ownership of enterprises, labour intensive and adapted technology, skills acquired outside the formal school system, and unregulated and competitive markets. The formal sector has reverse characteristics.

Although ILO's definition is the most important in the literature, there have been variations regarding which yardstick to use to identify small-scale producers. However, as Schmitz points out, the most widely applied definition is based on the size of the labour force: up to ten workers (Schmitz, 1982). Although there are also variations regarding the definition of the exact number of workers, Schmitz suggests that the different definitions of small-scale production by and large refer to the same group of agents (Schmitz, 1982).

As Moser and Schmitz show, the ILO Kenya mission was the most influential force in highlighting the importance of small-scale producers, inspiring several studies that took place in different parts of the world (Moser, 1984; Schmitz, 1982). The work of the ILO and the propagation of the informal sector concept were a great step forward because at that time the literature on employment was concerned with measuring under- and unemployment (Bienefeld and Godfrey, 1975; Schmitz, 1982). The ILO mission, on the contrary, concentrated on the actual activities of those who were classified as under/unemployed in the formal sector. It highlighted that small-scale units of production do not play a marginal or dead role in the economy, and are actually engaged in productive activities, which are pictured as being independent of the activities of the formal sector. However, the concept also has problems, which include its sharp division of the urban economy into two sectors, its uselessness in assisting the drawing of general conclusions, the application of multiple units of analysis, the confusion between growth and expansion, and its inability to explain the issue of growth properly.

The dualist view of the urban economy fails to acknowledge intermediate stages between the two sectors of the economy. The concept of two broad sectors makes it difficult to analyze each one. The empirical studies that have been conducted regarding the informal sector in different cities, e.g. the ILO city missions (Moser, 1984), encountered many difficulties when trying to draw general conclusions, because the informal sector includes heterogeneous sets of activities and people, whose definition is imprecise and who have no identifiable, analytically useful common characteristics (Bienefeld and Godfrey, 1975, p.7).

Also, the idea of the informal sector being evolutionary, capable of growth (e.g. Moser, 1984) can be interpreted in different ways. If growth means the expansion of the sector as a whole, it implies its persistence. However, if it means the actual development of the individual small-scale units of production, its consequence is a fundamental change in the sector, for the units will cease to be small-scale. This is an important element in this book, which deals with policies related to one group of small-scale producers (those engaged in the building of low-cost housing), because the way in which they evolve affects their characteristics and their capacity to produce the given good. Related to this issue is the fact that, as Isik points out, the informal sector concept is incapable of grasping the interconnection between different types of producers. Following, it is also incapable of defining the dynamics and limitations on growth which derive from this interconnection (Isik, 1992). Such issues will be resumed below, specifically in relation to low-cost housing.

Housing

The assertions about small-scale housing production in developing countries within the liberal neo-classical approach are here divided into two main groups: one which advocates a fractional participation of small-scale producers in the supply of low-cost housing, and another which advocates a broader participation of these producers.

The assertion of the first group is part of a broader case in favour of the private sector in general as a solution to the housing problem in developing countries. This case is defined by Hamdi and Goethert as the *supporters' view* (Hamdi and Goethert, 1989). The advocates of private production recognize that small-scale builders already play an important role in providing housing which is affordable to the lower strata of the population, and should therefore be supported along with large-scale producers (e.g. Christian, 1987; Preparatory Group Participants of the Vienna Recommendations on Shelter and Urban Development, 1987; Stimpson, 1987; Strassman, 1988). As Christian, for instance, suggests,

> squatter settlements stand as eloquent testimony to the ability of the market to provide shelter. Individuals and small, informal sector contractors can and do build shelter units (Christian, 1987, p. 54).

The above authors present a clear case for the private sector in general. Other authors such as Ramachandran (former Secretary-General of the United Nations Centre for Human Settlements), Durand-Lasserve, Munro and Pfeifer are also in tune with the supporter's view, although conveying their arguments in a less obvious way (Durand-Lasserve, 1987; Munro, 1987; Pfeifer, 1987; Ramachandran, 1987).

The supporters' argument is that the state should not provide housing directly, but should sustain private production. Their view is based upon a critique of the poor overall performance of the public sector in low-cost housing provision (e.g. Kitay,

1987; Mayo *et al.* 1986; Preparatory Group Participants of the Vienna Recommendations on Shelter and Urban Development, 1987; Urban Edge, 1987). According to this view, its performance is dismal because the state creates subsidies in its housing programmes, which impose financial burdens and thus make it difficult to replicate the programmes in the future. These facts are aggravated by the deteriorating economic conditions in most developing countries, which make it imperative for governments to minimize their debts as much as possible, and refrain from making subsidies such as those regarding housing projects. Public intervention in housing production also leads to unfair competition vis-a-vis the private sector, thus hindering its development and its capacity to contribute to housing provision (Preparatory Group Participants of the Vienna Recommendations on Shelter and Urban Development, 1987; Renaud, 1987). Therefore, private production should be encouraged. Small-scale contractors are mentioned explicitly.

The second group of authors, in turn, recommend a stronger participation of the small-scale contractors, arguing that their characteristics are such that they are more adequately equipped to cater for the low-income market than large-scale producers. These authors emphasise that most of the low-cost housing in developing countries has been produced by small-scale builders, and, in some cases, also point out the failures of large-scale builders (e.g. Drakakis-Smith, 1981; Ganesan, 1982, 1983; Lintz, 1989; Moavenzadeh, 1987; Rakodi, 1991; Rasmussen, 1990; Richwine, 1987; Rodwin and Sanyal, 1987).

Despite their different views as to whether or not large-scale production plays a role in the supply of low-cost housing, the two assertions above highlighted share a common view regarding the nature of small-scale producers, and can both be said to adopt the liberal neo-classical approach. Both views conceptualize small-scale producers as autonomous and separated from large-scale producers. At the same time, cooperation between the different types of producers is regarded as beneficial. Both assertions also concur in stating that small-scale producers have a series of advantages which enable them to play an important role in the supply of low-cost housing, but at the same time face constraints which hinder them. Therefore, policy proposals are suggested, which aim to remove such constraints. These advantages, constraints and policies will now be examined in turn.

There are five groups of advantages put forward within the two assertions. First, the idea that small-scale builders are inventive and that this characteristic makes them superior when producing low-cost housing (Richwine, 1987; Strassman, 1988). The fact that in many cases small-scale producers do not have access to avant-garde technology indeed stimulates their inventiveness to sort out solutions using only a limited range of resources available locally. However, this fact does not guarantee that such solutions are more suitable. If they are cheaper or culturally more appropriate than the other solutions, they fall into other groups of advantages, which will be analyzed next. Moreover, there is no element in the process of production of small-scale builders which would give them a specific advantage in terms of inventiveness - in fact, it is the larger units which concentrate upon research and development activities.

The second advantage is flexible production (Drakakis-Smith, 1981; Durand-Lasserve, 1987; Ganesan, 1983; Rodwin and Sanyal, 1987; Stimpson, 1987;

Strassman, 1988). This seems indeed to be important in the construction of low-cost housing, considering that the demand is dispersed and diversified, as opposed to concentrated and uniform, which would favour standardized production. However, the above authors do not analyze which are the characteristics of the demand for low-cost housing that require flexible production, and do not explain what are the internal characteristics of small-scale producers which allow them to be flexible.

The third advantage is culturally adapted design. Richwine points out that the high-technology type of product delivered by large-scale, formal builders does not reach low-income people (Richwine, 1987). It is here inferred that this author is contrasting a Western type of housing delivered by these builders, with an indigenous type delivered by small-scale ones. However, on the one hand, there have been many attempts by the formal sector to adapt their design to the cultural patterns of different countries, which suggests that small-scale builders do not have an advantage in this field. On the other hand, the whole idea that poor people throughout the developing world reject Western-style housing has been questioned.

The fourth characteristic regards the close links between small-scale builders and their clients (Pfeifer, 1987). However, the benefit of this fact is not clear. The close connection between builders and clients might make it easier for the latter to participate in the decision-making process regarding the construction of his/her house. However, this procedure is questionable from the point-of-view of production, because the clients' interference is bound to disrupt the production process, thus affecting productivity.

The last point, low price of the product, is due to the fact that small-scale producers have lower profit margins, are non-regulated, do not pay taxes, have a minimal need for transport, consume less energy, and use fewer imported materials (Durand-Lasserve, 1987; Moavenzadeh, 1987; Richwine, 1987; Rodwin and Sanyal, 1987). Low price as an advantage for low-cost housing construction is acceptable, considering the income situation of the lower strata of the population throughout the developing world. However, the characteristics of the demand which require low costs are not analyzed by the above authors. The internal characteristics of the small-scale producers which allow them to produce at a lower price are not analyzed either.

In short, although pointing out a number of factors that give the small-scale contractors an edge in low-cost housing production, the above authors do not give a thorough explanation of why these advantages exist, nor of the characteristics of the demand which require them. This book suggests that it is sensible to infer that a flexible process of production and low price are actually beneficial to the production of low-cost housing, an issue developed in Chapter 3.

The liberal neo-classical approach also asserts that the small-scale producers are constrained by a series of problems, which need to be removed. Firstly, as suggested by the first group of authors analyzed before, government intervention (through direct production) may hinder the strengthening of private production (including small-scale production) because, through subsidies and lack of profits, it provides housing at a price level with which the private sector cannot compete. This may discourage the latter from investing further in production, which, in turn, would have increased their productivity and reduced the price of the product.

9

A second problem is lack of good managerial skills (Ganesan, 1982, 1983; Preparatory Group Participants of the Vienna Recommendations on Shelter and Urban Development, 1987; Rodwin and Sanyal, 1987; Strassman, 1988). External factors have also been mentioned (Durand-Lasserve, 1987; Ganesan, 1983; Lintz, 1989; Preparatory Group Participants of the Vienna Recommendations on Shelter and Urban Development, 1987; Richwine, 1987; Rodwin and Sanyal, 1987; Strassman, 1988). They include lack of access to: land, infrastructure, finance, building materials, skilled labour force, equipment and regular flow of work. Finally, legal aspects of the business, such as excessively high regulatory standards for the units of production and building and material standards have also been noted (Durand-Lasserve, 1987; Lintz, 1989; Moavenzadeh, 1987; Richwine, 1987; Rodwin and Sanyal, 1987; Strassman, 1988).

In order to overcome the above-mentioned problems, a series of policy proposals has been put forward. Some of them are vague, arguing for the support of small-scale producers in general terms (e.g. Munro, 1987; Ramachandran, 1990). Others are geared to overcome specific problems, such as the provision of managerial and labour training, land, infrastructure, finance, equipments, flow of work and building materials, lowering of regulations (Durand-Lasserve, 1987; Lintz, 1989; Preparatory Group Participants of the Vienna Recommendations on Shelter and Urban Development, 1987; Rodwin and Sanyal, 1987; Strassman, 1988). A policy of reduction of government intervention is strongly emphasised.

In the introduction of the liberal neo-classical approach, it was shown that the idea of small-scale production as evolutionary can be interpreted in different ways. Does it mean the expansion of the sector as a whole, or the growth of the individual units of production? It is here suggested that, all things being equal, the second case will not benefit low-income settlements. The argument in favour of small-scale producers suggests that they have intrinsic attributes which enable them to cater for a fraction or even for the totality of the low-income market, which cannot be reached by large-scale producers. Therefore, if the small-scale producers capitalize and turn into large-scale ones, they lose these attributes. This question has not been addressed within the liberal neo-classical approach, which explicitly adopts the idea of growth of small-scale producers.

The liberal neo-classical approach has also been·used in the analysis of the construction industry in developing countries. This analysis has important inferences to small-scale builders and low-cost housing production.

Construction industry

Small-scale production is encompassed within a broader concern with the pivotal role that the construction industry plays in a country's development (e.g. Drewer, 1975; Turin, 1973), and with the fact that the construction industry of a large number of developing countries is in a very elementary and underdeveloped stage, thus having to rely on foreign firms, and spend a large amount of foreign currency (e.g. UNCHS, 1981).

The construction industry is not homogeneous, but formed by different types of producers (e.g. Drewer, 1975; Henriod, 1984; Ofori, 1980, 1989; Turin, 1973). Some authors focus on small-scale producers specifically, highlighting that they have an important role to play in the development of the indigenous construction industry in developing countries. They are regarded as effective channels for introducing local entrepreneurs into the construction industry at the local/national level (e.g. Chinosa, 1982; Cortez, 1979; Edmonds and Miles, 1984). These authors are specifically concerned with the development of local resources. Under such circumstances, small-scale contractors should be supported, for they are local resources and constitute the embryo of an indigenous industry. This view regards small-scale producers as independent, in accordance with the liberal neo-classical approach.

This view of small-scale producers within the construction industry encompasses the idea that they face constraints which hinder their growth, including lack of good managerial skills, lack of access to advanced technology (which encompasses equipment, labour skills and materials), and government discrimination. Therefore, policy proposals are put forward in order to remove them. However, many of the factors which constrain the growth of small-scale builders are exactly the factors which, according to the liberal neo-classical approach, constrain these builders to increase their participation in the provision of shelter in low-income settlements. Thus, the view regarding the development of the construction industry reinforces the problem emphasised before: the policy proposals regarding small-scale low-cost housing suggested by the liberal neo-classical approach clearly seem to be helpful for builders, but they will, *ceteris paribus*, drive them away from the production of low-cost housing, once they open up possibilities for the builders to capitalize, thus losing the intrinsic capacity that they have to cater for the low-income market.

Another approach to small-scale production of low-cost housing, appropriate technology, has a different starting point from the liberal neo-classical one. Nevertheless, its conclusion is similar in its view of the factors which enable and those which constrain builders' production of low-cost housing, and related policies.

The appropriate technology approach

This approach originated from the understanding that there has been a growing hiatus between industrialized and developing countries, and that the type of industrialization of the former when applied to the latter failed to fulfil the initial hopes of fostering development and of solving their basic problems. Therefore, it was necessary to implement technologies specifically suited to the developing world.

The term appropriate technology is used by some authors (e.g. Jequier, 1976) to designate the type of technology above mentioned. However, different terms are also used in the same context, such as intermediate (e.g. Schumacher, 1973), alternative (Dickson, 1974), or small-scale technology (Jackson, 1971), among others. The different authors agree that there is a need to implement technologies which are small-scale, labour intensive, which use the locally available resources and renewable sources of energy, and which do not clash with cultural traditions. This group of authors has been described as the appropriate technology movement (e.g. Gilbert, 1982; Kaplinsky, 1990; Widiono, 1989). Their ideas will accordingly be referred here as the appropriate technology approach.

11

The emphasis on small-scale activities, ranging from self-help schemes to small-scale private units of production, is a central theme of the appropriate technology approach. It also depicts a sharp dual division in the system of production, similarly to the liberal neo-classical approach. However, contrary to the previous approach, it broadly regards the relation between small- and large-scale production as non-beneficial, because of the problems of the latter. Also, it defines the small-scale producers in a different way: fundamentally on the basis of the technology which they use - labour intensive, environmentally sound and culturally adapted.

Housing

The most prominent champion of the appropriate technology notion applied to housing is Turner (e.g. Turner, 1985, 1988a, 1988b; Turner and Fitcher, 1972). Although his basic concern is with self-help and community development schemes, his work also refers to small-scale builders in such types of projects in different developing countries (e.g. Turner, 1988a, 1988b). Turner goes further than merely highlighting the role of small-scale builders in low-income settlements, by putting forward the concept of the *habitat worker* (Turner, 1985), which overlaps with the concept of the *barefoot architect* (Bristol, 1991; Busuttil, 1987; Saini, 1985). Actually, both the habitat worker and barefoot architect are a small-scale builder, who, as Saini suggests, should substitute its often ill-equipped counterparts working in low-income settlements (Saini, 1985). Other references to small-scale producers as providers of low-cost housing include Goethert and Hamdi, Inyang, IT Building, Miles and Parker (Goethert and Hamdi, 1988; Inyang, 1987; IT Building, undated; Miles and Parker, 1984).

Similarly to the liberal neo-classical approach, the appropriate technology approach notes the advantages of small-scale builders for producing low-cost housing, the constraints that they face and policies to remove such constraints.

By comparing the small-scale builders with the large-scale ones, the advantages of the former surface: large-scale production is income concentrating, is urban and foreign biased , uses less efficient equipment, only delivers in large scale, is culturally disruptive and has higher prices. However, the appropriate technology approach does not provide a consistent explanation about these issues, nor about how the possible attributes of small-scale producers meet the specific characteristics of the demand for low-cost housing. Some of the factors above mentioned indeed constitute clear advantages for small-scale low-cost housing production (prices and volume of production). They will be elaborated in Chapters 2 and 3.

The constraints which hinder the expansion of small-scale low-cost housing provision put forward by the appropriate technology approach match those which have been put forward by the liberal neo-classical approach. For instance, one of the premises of the barefoot architect concept is the fact that the current small-scale builders involved in low-cost housing production lack good management skills and equipment, which justifies the setting up of a scheme to train and equip new builders. Other authors such as Inyang also highlight the above problems, as well as the fact that small-scale producers also lack capital and skilled labour, and have to face regulatory constraints (e.g. Inyang, 1987). However, like the liberal neo-classical, the appropriate technology approach does not elaborate as to why and how the above factors actually constitute problems for small-scale producers.

In order to overcome the constraints faced by these producers, this approach puts forward a series of policy proposals similar to those emphasised by the liberal neo-classical authors. However, as already shown, the advantages of these policies for the production of low-cost housing is debatable. In this respect, the appropriate technology argument has a major flow, which regards profitability.

Although the appropriate technology movement does not suggest the overthrow of the capitalist system, it does not consider profitability, an issue which is at the heart of the system. However, the private producers are the decision-makers regarding, among other things, which kind of technology to use. They are likely to choose technologies which enhance their profits. They do not have any special commitment to a given type of technology just because it might contribute to the development of a country, or benefit a certain part of the population. As mentioned in the introduction, it is *business as usual*.

Gilbert, for instance, links the process of technological change in a capitalist society with a basic drive to increase profitability, and suggests that

> to eliminate the mechanism of profitability inspired technological change would call for the extinction of the profit motivated private firm and hence a change in the economic system as a whole, a revolutionary doctrine not espoused by the [appropriate technology] argument (Gilbert, 1982, p. 180).

In order to keep up with competition, producers have to transfer technologies from other successful producers and/or create new ones. However, if the producers' aim is success in the market place, one can ask why they should limit their choice of technology to the range of those considered appropriate to the country as a whole, if other types can fulfil this aim more effectively.

These considerations, on the one hand, expose shortcomings in the appropriate technology argument. On the other hand, they cast doubt on the effects of the policies put forward in support of small-scale, low-cost housing producers. Assuming that producers are the decision-makers and are basically profit-oriented, it is reasonable to expect that they will utilize the support received to reach their aims, and not necessarily to expand their production of low-cost housing.

There are other approaches to small-scale provision of low-cost housing, which see the subject from a different angle. Rather than emphasising the separation between small- and large-scale production and the characteristics of the unit of production such as technology, these approaches conceptualize small-scale producers as non-capitalists, and emphasise their links with capitalist producers. These approaches will be analyzed sequentially.

Modes of production

This approach focuses on the coexistence and articulation between different modes of production within a given social formation. This book deals with the concepts of

13

modes of production and social formation only to the extent of explaining their connection with small-scale housing production.

A mode of production has been defined as the combination of a given type of ownership of the means of production, a given form of appropriation of the economic surplus, a given degree of the development of the division of labour, and a given level of development of the forces of production (e.g. Laclau, 1971). Means of production are the material requirements of production, excluding living labour. They consist of instruments and subjects of labour. Instruments of labour refer to tools, plant and/or machinery, i.e. man-made utensils used for production - henceforth, instruments of labour will be referred as equipment. Subjects of labour are the materials manipulated and altered by labour. Forces of production, in turn, refer to the combination of the elements of the labour process (raw materials, means of production, labour force), or, more broadly, to the stage of material production in a given society.

Social formation entails either an empirical concept indicating the object of a tangible historical analysis (such as England in 1860, France in 1870, Russia in 1917), or an abstract concept which substitutes the idea of society and denotes the object of the science of history as the entirety of situations connected on the basis of a given mode of production (Balibar, 1966). Balibar also notes that concrete social formations by and large accommodate several distinct modes of production (Balibar, 1966). The modes of production approach has been applied to the analysis of developing countries (e.g. Bettelheim, 1972; Laclau, 1971; Quijano, 1974; Taylor, 1979; Terray, 1972; Vercruijsse, 1984; Wolpe, 1980). As Burgess notes, the development of the capitalist mode of production in Third World social formations takes place not by destroying pre-capitalist structures, but by modifying and reproducing them (Burgess, 1992). Within the modes of production approach, unlike the approaches analyzed previously, a given type of unit of production is not seen as belonging to a given sector of the economy such as the in/formal, nor as producing appropriate or modern technology. Emphasis is on its identification with a given mode of production, and its articulation with other types of units and modes.

The modes of production approach embodies the idea of change from one mode to another (e.g. Godelier, 1978). Related to the idea of change in the modes of production is the idea of change within units of production, for, as Wolpe suggests, a mode of production is intrinsically related to the structure of the individual units of production (Wolpe, 1980). Taylor, in turn, focuses specifically on the unit of production, suggesting the possibility of development of artisans when there are no constraints (Taylor, 1979). The notion of transformation in the modes of production and, consequently, in units of production, is important for this book, which focuses on the possibilities of transformation of one type of unit of production - i.e. small-scale builders.

Housing

The application of the approach to housing in general includes the concepts of forms of housing production (Cardoso and Short, 1983), and structures of housing provision, later expanded to structures of building provision ((Ball, 1983, 1986). Cardoso and Short's forms of housing production are described as combinations of conditions of

14

production, elements of labour process, and relations of production which are articulated through a specific network of agents (such as builders, labourers, developers, consumers) (Cardoso and Short, 1983).

The concept is explicitly based on the modes of production view, and recognizes the coexistence of different forms of housing production in a single social formation. These authors highlight the predominant existence of small-scale units of production in one of the forms: the individual contract production form. They also state the existence of a logical evolutionary pattern towards a pure capitalist form of housing production, implying the idea of change (Cardoso and Short, 1983). However, while the present book is specifically concerned with the changes in the internal structure of one agent (the builder/unit of production), such changes are just mentioned by Cardoso and Short briefly, and it is not known how and under which circumstances they occur.

Ball, who puts forward the concept of structures of housing provision, criticizes Cardoso and Short's concept for its vagueness in many respects. Ball's structure of housing provision characterizes a historical process of provision and reproduction of the physical (housing) entity. It focuses on the social agents essential to that process and the relations between them (Ball, 1983, 1986).

He uses the modes of production approach by acknowledging the possibility of different modes coexisting and being subordinated to capitalism. The notion of the coexistence of different modes is reflected in the notion of the coexistence of different structures of housing/building provision. The idea of contradictions within a mode of production leading to change is also applied by Ball - i.e. contradictions within a structure of production, leading to change.

Ball's concept is significant to this book for two reasons. Firstly, he suggests that change in a structure of production may occur not only through its contradictions, but also through political action. This point is important here in that it implies that policies, being political actions, may entail change. Therefore, they may result in a change in, rather than a reinforcement of, the process of small-scale low-cost housing production. Secondly, Ball relates the overall changes in housing provision to the specific inner transformation of the unit of production, which is the focus of this book.

However, Ball's argument has limitations in relation to the specific analysis of small-scale, low-cost housing production. Although referring to the transformation within the unit of production, he does not analyze it, nor refer to it except in the context of capitalist units. Also, it is difficult to link the overall changes in one structure of provision to specific changes in one type of builder, because Ball supports the possibility of the same category of builders operating in different structures.

The modes of production approach has also been applied specifically to the study of small-scale low-cost housing production in developing countries (Burgess, 1992; Isik, 1992; Tuffs, 1987). Isik studies speculative housing building in Turkey, which, according to him, is carried out by small-scale units of production (Isik, 1992). Tuffs focuses on small-scale low-cost housing production in Malaysia, and suggests that Taylor's development of the modes of production approach is worth applying in this area of study (Tuffs, 1987). Burgess suggests that the housing policies implemented by international and governmental agencies from the mid-1970s onwards in developing countries are based on an acceptance of the modes of production approach. The aim of such policies was still to enforce capitalist penetration (like previous policies), but now through a gradual process, using the articulation between capitalist and pre-capitalist modes, rather than by eliminating the latter immediately (Burgess, 1992).

Burgess stressed the existence of a widespread use of contracted builders in self-help housing schemes. This entailed an expansion of the capitalist relations of production, for, instead of building the house him/herself, the dweller hired the services of someone else. Burgess goes on to argue that the policies which support small-scale builders (e.g. by interfering in their traditional techniques, labour processes and materials) lead to their capitalization. This, in turn, increases the cost of housing to the final consumer, and

> put[s] the [housing] projects beyond the access of the majority of those housed in artisanal settlements and could seriously prejudice the livelihoods of many of the households in project areas (Burgess, 1992, p. 86).

This assertion is important here, in associating support policies with the capitalization of builders, and in showing their detrimental effect on low-cost housing production. However, although the above points are useful for this book, Burgess fails in his conceptualization of small-scale builders as labourers (i.e. not producers), in his lack of analysis of their capacity to produce low-cost housing and of the problems of their capitalization, and in his conceptualization of builders as pre-capitalist agents.

The analysis of Burgess and the other authors presented in this section reveals that, although there is no specific reference to a mode of production which is directly related to small-scale producers, the modes of production approach in general and in its particular application to housing embodies the idea of transformation, which is a central element of this book. It also embodies the idea of constraints which prevent a given mode of production or a form/structure of housing production/provision from changing. Such constraints can eventually be overcome, either through the enhancement of their internal contradictions, or through political action. Assuming the existence of a mode, form or structure which is based on small-scale production, the above analysis suggests that actions in support of these producers, emphasised in the previous sections, can open up possibilities of transformation/capitalization to them. This approach is beneficial in relation to those analyzed before, still based on a dual concept of the system of production. By not using a dual concept, the modes of production approach avoids gross generalizations and single policy proposals for two pseudo-uniform sectors, and facilitates the understanding of the process of growth.

However, the modes of production approach is nevertheless defective as a basis for the study of the role and growth of small-scale low-cost housing producers. It blurs the linkage between modes and units of production, its depiction of small-scale producers as pre-capitalists is inadequate for the analysis of developing countries (e.g. Aguiar Jr., 1989; Rudra, 1988), and it fails to describe the factors which enable the producers to build low-cost housing.

The concept of articulation of modes of production also has been used by another group of authors to stress the relations of exploitation between units of production. This idea is a relevant approach within the small-scale production literature, here termed transfer of surplus.

16

Transfer of surplus

The basic idea of this approach is the relation of exploitation between large-scale capitalist producers, on the one hand, and small-scale non-capitalist producers, on the other, through transfer of surplus. This relation hinders the development of the latter type of producers. Small-scale producers lose their capital, which is remitted directly to large-scale producers through financial and/or political channels; or they are prevented from accumulating it in the first place, by selling cheap goods for wage-workers employed in large-scale units. The sale of wage goods at a low price prevents them from collecting surplus. At the same time, this lowers the cost of the reproduction of labour power to the large-scale units, thus contributing to the expansion of their accumulation (e.g. Castells and Portes, 1989; Kowarick, 1979; Leys, 1975; Meillassoux, 1980; Nun et al., 1978; Oliveira, 1972; Prandi, 1978; Santos, 1979).

As Schmitz notes, the notion of transfer of surplus via direct remittance and sale of cheap goods for wage-workers embodies an explanation of the existence/persistence of small-scale producers (e.g. Schmitz, 1982). In a social formation dominated by a capitalist system prone to develop the forces of production, these producers should be condemned to extinction. However, they acquire a role in this context, in contributing to the accumulation of capitalist units of production (thorough the transfer of surplus). This idea separates the transfer of surplus from the modes of production approach.

The transfer of surplus approach has been important in identifying the possible harmful effects of policies related to small-scale production, which were not discussed by their advocates (analyzed before). One example, related to the sale of cheap goods, is that support for the establishment of small-scale units and the self-help schemes which supply them actually results in the provision of low-quality products for the working-class. Another example, related to the notion of direct remittance, is the increasingly common practice in larger units of production of subcontracting external labour rather than having in-house employees. Although the subcontracted worker may earn more than a wage-worker, and have the sensation of independence from a labour hierarchy, the medium/long-term effects include instability in the demand for his/her work, increased expenditure on health care and other (ex)social security benefits, as well as the weakening of trade unions and a reduction in bargaining power (e.g. Castells and Portes, 1989).

Housing

Reference to the direct remittance of surplus between small- and large-scale producers in the house-building sector is made, for instance, by Lanzetta and Murillo, who analyze subcontracting procedures in Colombia (Lanzetta and Murillo, 1989). Reference to the sale of cheap goods in broad terms is made by a number of authors who stress the usefulness of squatter settlements in capitalist societies, as being an inexpensive housing solution (e.g. Castells, 1980; Castells and Portes, 1989; Collier, 1976). Other authors are more specific, in emphasising the production process - i.e. that self-help housing is a means of lowering the costs of the reproduction of labour power (e.g. Bonduki and Rolnick, 1979; Harms, 1982; Maricato, 1987). It is important to note that self-help housing implies not only the construction carried out by the dweller alone and/or with the help of relatives and friends, but also the use of paid labour (e.g. Burgess, 1992; Drakakis-Smith, 1981; Mautner, 1989; Moser, 1982). The transfer of surplus approach has problems both on a general level and when applied to low-cost housing. For instance, Schmitz provided empirical evidence to suggest that there are broad variations in the types of goods consumed by wage-workers. While in some African cities such goods were indeed produced by small-scale/artisanal units (confirming the transfer of surplus idea), in other cases, as in many Latin American cities, such goods were mainly produced by large-scale/industrialized units (Schmitz, 1982). Thus, the notion of the sale of cheap goods cannot be generalized.

At the theoretical level, Schmitz suggests that the transfer of surplus approach

> turns the theory of capitalist accumulation on its head by positing a dependency on that part of the economy which is the least developed (Schmitz, 1982, p. 19).

Also, the transfer of surplus approach is still attached to the idea of a dual system of production, encompassing concepts such as the in/formal sector (e.g. Castells and Portes, 1989; Leys, 1975).

The question of the capacity of small-scale builders to produce low-cost housing, the constraints on them, related policies, and the process of development of such producers have not been fully explained within the transfer of surplus approach. In terms of the production of low-cost housing, this approach does not take into consideration the characteristics of small-scale builders. The analysis of their process of production could identify factors which would explain such characteristics. However, the transfer of surplus approach merely states that small-scale producers provide housing at lower prices, without explaining why.

Similarly, the approach does not tackle the question of the constraints that small-scale producers face in the construction of low-cost housing. The idea is that any constraint exists because the producers cannot retain their surplus, therefore cannot reinvest in their production process. This might affect both the present activities of the producers and the process of development. Consequently, the concept of the transfer of surplus approach about the process of development of small-scale producers actually emphasises their non-development, and does not advance any idea of how change could take place if surplus was retained. Such facts hinder the strength of the approach as a basis for analysis of the role and growth of small-scale low-cost housing producers.

The idea of articulation between different types of producers and/or modes of production has also been used by another body of authors, who stress the connection between a specific type of units of production - petty-commodity producers - and capitalist units.

Petty-commodity production

Petty-commodity production is a concept which, like modes of production, derives from Marx's theory of coexisting modes of production, and the linkages between them

(Marx, 1977). Contrary to the emphasis of the transfer of surplus approach on a connection between two sectors, petty-commodity production embraces the idea of connections within a system of production constituted by several sectors. This is similar to the modes of production approach. However, it differs from the modes of production approach for depicting the connection at the level of the unit of production, highlighting the existence of a continuum ranging from petty-commodity production, on the one side, and full capitalist production, on the other. From the 1970s onwards, the petty-commodity production approach has been used to analyze small-scale activities in developing countries.

The petty-commodity production concept has been applied by one group of authors in a similar fashion to the argument of the transfer of surplus approach: petty-commodity production is useful to capitalism for lowering the costs of the reproduction of labour power, and/or for transferring surplus through subcontracting operations (e.g. Davies, 1979; Gerry, 1978, 1979; Gerry and Birkbeck, 1981; Le Brun and Gerry, 1975). The above position has been criticized by a number of authors, some of which belonging to the petty-commodity production approach itself (e.g. Ayatta, 1986; Basok, 1989; Bernstein, 1986, 1988; Gibson and Neocosmos, 1985; Long and Richardson, 1978; Scott, 1986a, 1986b). As an alternative to the emphasis on the usefulness of petty-commodity production to the capitalist system, these authors gave attention to the internal dynamics of the producers and their organization of production.

The idea that there are different possibilities for the relationship between petty-commodity and capitalist production is superior to the transfer of surplus and appropriate technology approaches (which overlook the possibility of a beneficial relationship between the two sets of producers), and is also superior to the liberal neo-classical approach (which overlooks the detrimental relationship). Although recognizing that petty-commodity production is linked to the capitalist system in general, attention is shifted from its external to its internal relations. This position is important to this book, which needs to study the inner aspects of small-scale producers, in order to explain why they are well adapted to provide low-cost housing, what are they constraints to grow, and what happens when such constraints are removed. A number of authors who have made a cross-sectional study of petty-commodity production in different countries highlight the way it meets the needs of the poor (e.g. Bienefeld, 1979; Gerry, 1979; Le Brun and Gerry, 1975; Scott, 1979). Also, as Moser shows, the petty-commodity production approach is able to identify the constraints that prevent small-scale producers from developing (Moser, 1984). The approach goes even further, by focusing on the possibilities of overcoming such constraints, which leads to the transformation and capitalization of producers (Basok, 1989; Bernstein, 1986, 1988; Bienefeld, 1979; Blincow, 1986; Gerry, 1978, 1979; Gibson and Neocosmos, 1985; Le Brun and Gerry, 1975; Levin and Neocosmos, 1989; Long and Richardson, 1978; Scott, 1979, 1986a, 1986b).

Housing

The petty-commodity production approach examines attributes which enable the builders to produce low-cost housing. This analysis is based on findings from

19

Tanzania and Kenya (Bienefeld, 1979), Malaysia (Johnstone, 1984), Senegal (Le Brun and Gerry, 1975) and Peru (Scott, 1979). The aggregate conclusion is that petty-commodity builders survive in markets which are unprofitable for capitalist builders. Due to the size of these markets, their risks and the uncertainties of demand, capitalist producers are unable to take advantage of mass-production and economies of scale. However, petty-commodity producers have the flexibility to cope with those markets' variations. Also, petty-commodity producers provide housing at a lower price than capitalist ones. A basic benefit of mass-production and economies of scale is cost reduction. Without this scheme of production, capitalist units cannot rival petty-commodity ones in terms of costs (see the discussion on machinofacture and fordism, in Chapter 2).

The petty-commodity production approach also focuses on the constraints that hinder builders from capitalization, such as lack of access to machinery, lack of access to credit, unstable markets, illiteracy (Burgess, 1978, 1982; Gerry, 1978; Mautner, 1987, 1989, 1991).

This approach also points out the possibilities of removing such constraints. Bienefeld, Gerry and Le Brun, for instance, note the increasing establishment of capitalist relations of production in petty-commodity production units (Bienefeld, 1979; Gerry, 1978; Le Brun and Gerry, 1975). Gilbert also emphasises the issue of constraints on growth, and goes even further, connecting it to the effects on low-cost housing production. He suggests that the removal of the constraints faced by petty-commodity producers will increase the price of low-cost housing (Gilbert, 1986). The idea is that petty-commodity producers provide affordable housing for the low-income population, and, if they capitalize, their costs of production for this specific type of housing will increase. This point needs elaboration to show why capitalist producers cannot provide low-cost housing, even when they have higher productivity (this will be carried out in Chapter 2). Nevertheless, it shows that supporting the petty-commodity builders is not necessarily beneficial to their activities in low-income settlements.

Conclusion

This chapter has analyzed five approaches to small-scale production of low-cost housing in developing countries. Although having differences regarding the conceptualization of small-scale producers and their process of development, the liberal neo-classical and the appropriate technology approaches agree in relation to the fact that the small-scale contractors have a set of specific attributes which enable them to produce low-cost housing, face a set of constraints which hinder their activities, and that a set of policies should be implemented in order to remove such constraints. It is reasonable to believe that a number of the factors pointed out by these approaches indeed constitute attributes of the small-scale contractors, and other factors constitute constraints for their development. However, neither approach elaborates the issue efficiently. Both approaches have problems in their conceptualization of small-scale producers, which weakens their definitional power and obstructs their capacity to explain the dynamics of growth. The formulation of policies to support the builders entails a major problem: they open up growth possibilities for the builders, which might eliminate their constraints, but at the same time eliminate their capacity to produce low-cost housing.

The three other approaches analyzed in this chapter conceptualize small-scale contractors as non-capitalists, and emphasise their links with capitalist producers. The modes of production and the transfer of surplus approaches have weaknesses in depicting the attributes which enable the builders to produce low-cost housing, the constraints upon production and the effects of policies to remove such constraints. The petty-commodity production approach has been highlighted as containing elements which may form an effective basis for a theoretical framework to analyze these issues. This will be developed in the next chapter.

2 Non-capitalist production of low-cost housing in developing countries

This chapter starts by elaborating concepts which will be used as a basis for understanding the role of small-scale builders in low-cost housing production in developing countries: (i) the definition of petty-commodity production as a form of production, (ii) the definition of the object of the study (the small-scale builders) as petty-commodity producers, (iii) the definition of labour process, and (iv) the correlation between forms of production and labour processes. Following, the chapter examines the characteristics of the demand for low-cost housing and the characteristics of the process of production in which the builders are engaged. The two sets of characteristics are compared in order to show why these builders are able to produce low-cost housing. Finally, the chapter explains the notion of growth constraints faced by small-scale builders, and the possibilities of moving along the continuum towards capitalist production, when such constraints are removed.

Theoretical concepts

As already noted, the petty-commodity production concept will be used as a basis for the framework to be developed in this chapter. This framework will also be supported by supplementary theoretical elements, which will be used in order to expand the petty-commodity production concept - namely, the analysis of the development of the labour process in capitalism and general economic theory.

The petty-commodity form of production and the development of the labour process

It will be argued that the analysis of the labour processes of petty-commodity and capitalist producers unveils the factors which enable the former to build low-cost housing, and unveils the features of their capitalization. Therefore, in order to carry out the analysis, the association between different forms of production and labour processes, as well as the transition from one form of production and labour process to another will be explained.

Petty-commodity production is here conceptualized as a form of production. This is supported by a number of authors noted in Chapter 1, who use the petty-commodity production concept in this way (e.g. Basok, 1989; Gerry, 1979; Le Brun and Gerry, 1975; Scott, 1986a, 1986b; Smith, 1986).

Scott gives a comprehensive view of forms of production, referring specifically to the process of production *at the level of the unit of production*. She defines forms of production in terms of the technical and social relations embodied in the process of production of the unit of production, resulting in the creation and appropriation of surplus labour (Scott, 1986b). This definition is adopted in this book.

Social relations of production refer to relations between the owners of the means of production and the direct producers. In terms of the social relations, petty-commodity production is characterized by the ownership of the means of production by the direct producers, and by little separation between labour and capital (e.g. Bernstein, 1986, 1988; Gibson and Neocosmos, 1985; Levin and Neocosmos, 1989; Long and Richardson, 1978; Scott, 1979, 1986b).

Technical relations of production, in turn, refer to the relations between the agents of production (the individuals involved in production) and the means of production - i.e. the technical characteristics of the labour process. Petty-commodity production is characterized by a labour process which entails low division of labour, little specialization and small-scale production (Ball, 1988a), and small size of the workforce (Bromley, 1985; Burgess, 1982; Mautner, 1987).

Small-scale builders who produce low-cost housing in developing countries are defined in this study as petty-commodity producers, encompassing the characteristics outlined in the previous paragraphs.

The labour process of a given producer can be organized in different ways, according to the type and interplay of its elements. According to Scott (1986b), a given labour process is associated with a given form of production. Therefore, a given labour process, to be examined later, is associated with petty-commodity production.

Capitalism is, at the same time, related to a mode and a form of production. It refers to the way a given society is organized, including its economic, political and ideological elements - mode of production. But it also entails the technical and social relations at the level of the unit of production - form of production. Similarly to petty-commodity production, a given labour process (or processes) is (are) associated with capitalist production.

The petty-commodity production concept includes the notion of a continuum ranging from petty-commodity to full-capitalist production. It is here suggested that this continuum also exists at the level of the labour process, ranging from handicraft to manufacture, and then to machinofacture (also called large-scale or modern industry), and post-fordism (which will be explained later). Petty-commodity production entails a handicraft labour process. Capitalist production entails an elementary stage of manufacture. Finally, advanced capitalist production entails an advanced stage of manufacture, elementary machinofacture, advanced machinofacture (fordism) and post-fordism. The term advanced capitalist production has been used in a general sense to differentiate between further stages of capitalism from its initial form. Nevertheless, it is here acknowledged that capitalist production advances continuously, as the labour process changes.

23

The above associations do not cover the whole universe of possibilities. A given labour process may be related to other forms and modes of production - for instance, handicraft in feudalism. Besides this, the passage from petty-commodity to capitalist production does not represent the only feasible progression for a given unit of production. For instance, according to the circumstances, it is also possible that a capitalist unit goes back to a petty-commodity production stage. Also, a petty-commodity producer might stagnate or become a proletarian. However, the aim here is not to explore the full range of alternatives, but *to analyze the specific passage from the stage of handicraft petty-commodity production to elementary manufacture capitalist production, then to advanced manufacture and finally to machinofacture advanced capitalism.*

Manufacture is defined as the labour process in which capitalist production originates. The previous process, handicraft (or artisanal production), is characterized by lack of division of labour. The artisan, although sometimes helped by apprentices and/or journeymen, is directly responsible for all the stages of the production process (e.g. Fundação João Pinheiro, 1984). There is no wage-work - a fundamental characteristic of capitalism - involved in handicraft. Le Brun and Gerry clarify this issue, showing that the journeyman is not a wage-worker because he receives certain shares of revenues, and uses the means of production for personal earnings. The wage-worker, in turn, generally does not have any share in revenues, and is completely alienated from the means of production (Le Brun and Gerry, 1975). Another differentiating aspect is the period of permanence in the unit of production. While the wage-worker is usually hired on a regular basis to carry out activities through a period of months or years, the journeyman sells his labour-power on a free lance basis, undertaking casual assignments.

Handicraft is also characterized by small-scale production, as opposed to the subsequent labour processes. Marx points out that capitalist production actually starts when the owner of the unit of production hires a large number of labourers (i.e. large in comparison to handicraft production). The initial capitalist labour process is carried out on a larger scale and generates a large quantity of products (Marx, 1977). Handicraft is a labour process associated with petty-commodity production, and the passage from handicraft to manufacture entails a passage from petty-commodity to capitalist production. There are also transformations within manufacture, from an elementary to an advanced stage, which correspond to a transformation in capitalist production. In order to understand such passages, the transformations in manufacture will be explained.

Manufacture is a form of cooperation entailing division of labour, still based in handicraft production, but which involves a differentiation between capitalists and wage-workers - thus constituting a capitalist labour process. Manufacture originates by assembling labourers together in a workshop under the control of a capitalist. This can take place in two ways. First, labourers belonging to different independent crafts, through whose hands a given article must pass on its way to completion. Second, labourers belonging to the same craft, who perform the same activities (e.g. Liberaki, 1988; Marx, 1977). In both situations, the case is to put together labourers who were working apart. However, there is a specialization of the labour process in manufacture (Liberaki, 1988; Marx, 1977).

24

The elementary stage of manufacture embodies the onset of capitalist production. In this stage, the producer can be directly involved in some phases of the work - therefore being an artisan - but in other phases s/he supervises a small group of wage-labourers - thus representing capital. As manufacture develops, and so division of labour, the stages in which the producer supervises wage-labourers increasingly supersede those in which s/he works as artisan. Thus, there is an increasing capitalization of production. This process is not restricted to technical aspects, as it also entails social change. However, this book concentrates on the transformations within the unit of production.

There is also a transitional phase in the passage between manufacture and machinofacture. The latter is characterized by the central part played by machinery, which substitutes manual work and tools - manufacture, the previous process, means *made by hand*, whereas machinofacture means *made by machine*. The introduction of machinery does not occur overnight either, but gradually (e.g. Liberaki, 1988).

Machinofacture has two stages of development: the assembling of analogous and simultaneous functioning machines; and the connection of different machines in the production process, each one being responsible for a part of a product. In machinofacture, the production process is not interrupted by the intervention of the labourer, who is de-skilled. In this labour process there is a further increase in the scale of production (e.g. Brighton Labour Process Group, 1977), which is bolstered by the widespread use of machinery - the larger and more complex the machine, the less divisible it becomes, therefore necessitating a larger output in order to be worth using. The output produced by each machine or set of machines is standardized, for machinery is designed for special purposes.

The production of standardized outputs at large-scale is further increased with the advent of fordism, which is an advanced stage of machinofacture. As Harvey suggests, fordism entails a new form of economic organization, or a regime of accumulation (e.g. Harvey, 1989). However, for the purpose of this book, it will be analyzed only at the level of the labour process. In this context, fordism regards production based on the innovations proposed by Henry Ford - e.g. the moving production lines with conveyor belts, which tightened the connection between different machines and phases of production (e.g. Harvey, 1989; Liberaki, 1988; Vargas, 1979). As Liberaki suggests, it is primarily concerned with cost-reduction, a fact which leads towards a continuous standardization of products, the use of special-purpose machinery, and the increase in economies of scale (Liberaki, 1988).

Above are the basic features of machinofacture. However, the development of the labour process did not stop at this stage. The past few decades have witnessed the proliferation of units of production different from the mass-producing/conveyor-belt type. They are based on a process which has broadly been termed post-fordist. Like fordism, it has been associated with a new form of economic organization, or a regime of accumulation (e.g. Jessop, 1990; Lovering, 1991). Other terms have been used to analyze the changes which have been occurring in production, such as systemofacture (e.g. Kaplinsky, 1985), flexible specialization (Piore and Sabel, 1984), flexible accumulation (Harvey, 1989). However, post-fordism is the term most widely applied, and, for the sake of simplification, it will be used here in reference to the recent trends in production.

25

Although there are variations in post-fordism, its basic characteristics *at the level of production* entail a reorganization of the workforce intra-firm, with re-skilling, a large level of cooperation between units and/or subcontracting, the substitution of machines which can deliver only one product for flexible machinery, usually equipped with electronic systems, which can deliver different ones (e.g. Kaplinsky, 1990; Liberaki, 1988; Schmitz, 1989). Research carried out in Europe and the U.S.A. has shown that construction firms have also embraced post-fordist elements, moving away from the 'large-scale concrete systems devised for the mega-housing projects of the 1960s' (Ball, 1988b, p. 170), when the goal was to reduce housing production as much as possible to 'Fordist' style mass-production virtually identical to that of motor cars' (Ball, 1988b, p. 191). The post-fordist tendencies in housing construction include greater fragmentation of the construction process, detailed management accounting control, a greater use of subcontracted labour and equipment (Ball, 1988b; Bonke and Jensen, 1982; Harloe, 1988; Werna, 1994). There is evidence that such tendencies have also penetrated the developing world, at least in new industrializing countries such as Brazil (e.g. IPT, 1988).

Post-fordism is still linked with large-scale production, due to the scale of most flexible machinery (e.g. Sayer, 1988; Schonberger, 1988), and the continuing need for economies of scale and a large quantity of output (Gertler, 1988; Sayer, 1988). However, there is more scope for participation of small-scale units of production. Subcontracting, although existent in machinofacture, is much more developed in the subsequent process (e.g. Liberaki, 1988; Piore and Sabel, 1984; Schmitz, 1989). Moreover, there are also cases in which a number of small-scale units work together, in a complex system of reciprocal subcontracting, without the existence of a parent/large-scale unit (Liberaki, 1988).

Having introduced the role of small-scale producers in post-fordism, it is important to point out their difference from petty-commodity artisanal producers. This issue is emphasised by Scott. She takes the example of self-employed producers of computer software, and suggests that they could not be included in Marx's category of petty-commodity producers, for they take part in an intricate division of labour within the industry, and work with advanced forces of production (Scott, 1986b). In the specific case of the construction industry, the post-fordist tendencies include a shift from site to factory activities. Site operations are reduced as much ·as possible to the assembly of pre-fabricated components (e.g. Ball, 1988b), using sophisticated equipment. Petty-commodity production, on the other hand, is still heavily based on site activities and on the use of elementary tools.

Post-fordism has been emphasised above to give a more comprehensive view of the development of production in general and of the labour process in particular. However, this book is specifically concerned with the transition from handicraft to different stages of manufacture, and with the transition from manufacture to machinofacture. The following sections will focus on these issues.

To summarize the present section, petty-commodity production is defined as a form of production, to which corresponds the artisanal labour process. Capitalist production corresponds, at the same time, to a form and a mode of production, and is associated, in broad terms, with the labour processes of manufacture, elementary machinofacture, advanced machinofacture (fordism), and post-fordism. There is a continuum connecting the different forms of production and labour processes, which is summarized in Table 2.1. This continuum presents the stages through which a petty-commodity producer passes in its process of growth.

Table 2.1
Conceptual model of the continuum of production including form of production and labour process

labour	PCP	Handicraft
process	CP	Elementary manufacture
	ACP	Advanced manufacture, machinofacture and post-fordism

Key:

PCP - petty-commodity production
CP - capitalist production
ACP - advanced capitalist production

The analysis of the labour processes is important because it unveils the factors which enable petty-commodity producers to build low-cost housing, and how they change as the producers move along the continuum towards capitalist production. But in order to understand why petty-commodity builders are capable of producing low-cost urban housing in developing countries, the characteristics of the demand need to be analyzed.

The demand for low-cost urban housing in developing countries

Low-cost urban housing refers to housing produced for the consumption of low-income people in cities and towns, i.e. to the urban poor. Definitions of poverty vary, for instance, according to household income, consumption in general terms, food consumption, food ration, calories, medical data, basic needs (e.g. Glewwe and Van der Gaag, 1990). However, there are great overlaps between the groups of people defined through the different yardsticks (for example, those with lower consumption of food generally are the same people who have more health problems, lower incomes, etc). The characteristics of the demand for low-cost housing throughout the developing world also vary. Part of the urban poor may be able to purchase finished dwellings. Other groups of urban poor may be lucky enough to build their houses completely without any paid labour. However, on the one hand, there is ample evidence that most schemes (either public or private) to sell finished housing for the poor throughout the developing world have failed. On the other hand, by and large the urban poor do no have the know-how and also the time to carry out *all* stages of the building process, especially if this process entails technical expertise to deal with bricks, concrete, ceramic or asbestos roof, finishing work, installations, among many others issues.

Also, relatives or friends who have both the know-how and availability are scant (e.g. Inyang, 1987). Thus, they have resorted to small-scale private contractors to carry out at least the most significant parts of the building process - and often the entire process (e.g. Bienefeld, 1979; Burgess, 1992; IBAM, 1982, 1986; Inyang, 1987; Johnstone, 1978, 1984; Maricato, 1987; Mautner, 1987, 1989, 1991; Ozuekren, 1989; PADCO/USAID, 1985; Phillip, 1987; Rakodi, 1989; Rasmussen, 1990; Taschner and Mautner, 1982; Tuffs, 1987; Wycliffe, 1987).

In order to produce low-cost housing, such builders have to be prepared to meet a demand which is *diversified, discontinuous, small-scale and capable only of atomized disbursements*. The houses are built piecemeal, with frequent interruptions. The dwellers cannot pay for the whole construction continuously. They face the gravest budget problems among all strata in society, and look for the cheapest housing at the standards of construction which currently prevail in low-income settlements.

The issue of diversity of demand for housing has been noted by Burgess and Pradilla, among others. They stress the dominance of and/or preference for individualized rather than standardized housing (Burgess, 1978, 1982; Pradilla, 1976). The financial constraints of the low-income dwellers have been noted, for instance, by authors who have argued in favour of self-help housing (which encompasses the work of small-scale builders). The argument is that in self-help schemes the low-income dwellers can build according to the pace they can afford (e.g. Ward, 1982); a fact which suggests the existence of variations and discontinuities in the construction process, once a large portion of the poor face fluctuations in their system of income generation (e.g. Bruce and Dwyer, 1988). This situation also drives the poor to demand small-scale services, once they cannot afford major undertakings in one go.

Primary data collected in the city of Belo Horizonte, Brazil, confirms the above reasoning. Rosa, for instance, is a fifty-two years old house-cleaner, who lives with her sixty-one years old retired husband. Throughout their whole life they lived in rental accommodation. In 1987 they managed to buy a plot of land in the Ouro Preto neighbourhood, out of their savings and with the financial help of their grown-up offspring. Three years later, their 40 square meters house was under construction. Rosa gave the following statement:

> All the money I earn is spent on the house... My husband receives a pension, that is how we have been living. Sometimes we do not have enough food to eat, and we have to rely on help from our relatives or neighbours. But that is the only way we can manage to build the house.. Sometimes we save so little that we can only hire a builder for less than a week. But we prefer to do it little by little... If we save the money to do it later in one-go, a 'surprise' government programme or the inflation might eat it up - we rather spend it right away.

Margarida is a forty years-old divorced seamstress who lives with her six children in a 60 square meters house in the Agua Branca neighbourhood. She bought the plot of land containing a little shack more than twenty years ago. Her present house has been built bit-by-bit ever since by a number of builders. She states that

28

I have been living in this house for the past twenty years, and still have not been able to finish it completely. It has been hard for me to do it all in one-go... Sometimes I was able to pay a builder to do a lot, like when my husband changed jobs and got his security pension from the previous one, and when he was on health licence [thus still receiving his wages] but was working in parallel in something else... But in many other occasions things have been different. In many occasions one of my six children would tell me that he could not continue to go to school with his old sandals which were falling apart. This is the way we have been living... We have to sacrifice my own comfort and that of the children in order to build. But even so, in many occasions the situation got out-of-hand and then we had to stop the construction once more.

Jurandir, a forty-nine years-old factory porter, has bought a plot of land in the Ouro Preto neighbourhood. He declared that:

During the construction of my house, I was living in a nearby shack with my wife and five children... Now we live in the house, which, as you see, still needs the finishing to be carried out... I managed to hire a builder to build a lot during the two periods when I changed jobs, because of the pension, and, later on, with the help of some of my sons who started working... But even so, we had to stop ten times... The time between the stops varied from a few days to one month.

The dwellers/clients from sites-and-services schemes, such as in Confisco, benefited from government support - financing and provision of land and building materials. They had only to hire builders to carry out the construction of the houses. Even so, they had difficulties similar to those above described, and have similar characteristics of demand for housing. For instance, Neide, a forty-five years-old cook, has stated that:

Before coming here, I was living with my grown-up children. Now, finally, I have managed to acquire this house. But even with all the help from the government, it is not easy to build... I build according to my pocket, which many times is empty or almost empty... This means that I can only hire the builder for one week or so... Then he has to go, but we keep in touch; so, after a few weeks, when my condition is a bit better, he comes back again.

In sum, the above accounts confirm the characteristics of the demand for low-cost housing in developing countries stated by the authors mentioned in the beginning of this section: diversified, built in small and discontinuous stages, and capable only of atomized disbursements. Now, the way the petty-commodity builders respond to it will be analyzed.

The production of low-cost housing in developing countries

In order to build low-cost housing, the unit of production needs flexibility to provide small-scale services, to shift from the construction of one stage of a given house to the construction of another stage of another house, and needs to offer services at the lowest price consistent with the present standards of construction in low-income settlements. As shown in the previous chapter, petty-commodity producers have flexibility to cope with market variations, which cannot be met by a rigid production of standardized goods. They survive in markets in which, due to their small size, risks and uncertainties of demand, capitalist producers are not able to take advantage of mass-production/economies of scale (e.g. Bienefeld, 1979; Johnstone, 1984; Le Brun and Gerry, 1975; Scott, 1979).

In order to build low-cost housing, the unit of production needs flexibility at a *determinate level of prices*. A large-scale, capitalist unit of production is technically capable of meeting a diversified, small-scale and discontinuous demand. It has the labour skills and equipment to build, for instance, one wall in one house, and then shift to the roof in a second house, then to the foundations in a third one, and so on. However, to meet this type of demand, the prices of its services would be much higher than those of a petty-commodity builder. This happens because in markets with a demand like that of low-cost housing in developing countries, capitalist producers cannot benefit from mass production and economies of scale. The differences between petty-commodity and capitalist producers, and the way they respond (or not) to the demand for low-cost housing will be detailed in the next chapter, when the characteristics of the labour processes associated with the different forms of production are analyzed.

In sum, petty-commodity producers have the degree of flexibility and prices of their services to meet the specific characteristics of the demand for low-cost housing in developing countries. They are able to deliver discontinuous and small outputs of different goods at a lower price than capitalist producers. The emphasis on flexibility and prices in this book does not imply that the analysis of all the factors related to the capacity of petty-commodity builders to produce low-cost housing have been covered. However, the analysis developed here reveals that these specific factors have a pivotal importance. Having defined the attributes of the builders, their process of growth will be analyzed now.

The growth of the petty-commodity producers

This section examines the process of capitalization of petty-commodity producers, and the factors which influence it. Capitalization is not the only possible option open to petty-commodity producers. Thus, before analysing this process, an overall view of different possibilities will be given. They include the process of transformation into proletarians, expansion of petty-commodity production as a whole (which is different from the growth and capitalization of individual producers), and stagnation.

As Basok suggests, the trajectory of development of petty-commodity producers is connected to the constraints and opportunities created by the overall capitalist system

(Basok, 1989). Based on this assertion, it is here understood that the process of expansion or stagnation of petty-commodity producers is linked to specific opportunities and/or constraints on their activities, but is also linked to growth constraints. The existence of the latter type of constraints may keep a larger number of units in petty-commodity production.

At this point, it is necessary to stress that there are two types of constraints, both mentioned in the previous paragraph. First, those which hinder the present activities of petty-commodity producers, i.e. hinder their expansion. Second, those which hinder their process of capitalization. This book is concerned with the second.

Another possible option to petty-commodity production mentioned previously is their transformation into proletarians. This transformation along with capitalization correspond to the Marxian view of two polar processes of change for petty-commodity producers (e.g. Ayatta, 1986; Bernstein, 1986, 1988; Friedman, 1980; Gibson and Neocosmos, 1985; Neocosmos, 1986). Although accepting the existence of these two possibilities, this book emphasises that some petty-commodity producers do not have, necessarily, to become proletarians for others to capitalize. The advent of a new capitalist unit of production means, *ceteris paribus*, that new wage-labourers have to appear, to form the labour force of the unit. But the new labourers may come from different backgrounds, depending on the characteristics of the social formation - for instance, they may come from those engaged in domestic production, in agriculture, or from the natural growth of the proletariat. The process of transformation of petty-commodity producers into proletarians occurs in a context of constraints and opportunities peculiar to each social formation. It is also connected to the constraints on capitalization: it constitutes an alternative for those who are excluded from the process of growth.

Despite the different possible options to petty-commodity production, it is here suggested that petty-commodity producers aim at capitalizing. This idea derives from the assumption put forward in economic and political economic theory regarding the profit-orientation of capitalist producers (e.g. Lipsey, 1971; Marx, 1977). Albeit not being capitalist, petty-commodity producers operate in a milieu dominated by capitalism - whose main drive is accumulation - and are linked to capitalist production in many ways. If they do not save or accumulate, it is not for lack of motivation, but for the existence of constraints - which, if removed, open up possibilities for growth. Thus, the possibility or not of overcoming growth constraints will affect the path followed: whether capitalization, or one of the other aforementioned alternatives.

The capitalization of petty-commodity producers deriving from the removal of a number of constraints is supported in the literature (e.g. Basok, 1989; Bienefeld, 1979; Burgess, 1978, 1982; Gerry, 1978; Gogh, 1990; Le Brun and Gerry, 1975; Scott, 1979).

Based on these authors, it is here suggested that the growth of petty-commodity producers is linked to the removal of three groups of factors. First, blocked access to a number of elements related to the production process, which include equipment, materials, credit, and labour and managerial capacity. Second, low wage levels in the building industry. Third, factors related to the market for the goods supplied by the petty-commodity producers, including excessively high building standards, demand for individualized housing, lack of effective demand and excessive competition.

Instead of developing an aggregate examination of a large number of constraints, as has been commonly carried out in the small-scale production literature, this book follows a different path, which is to select pivotal constraints, and analyze them separately in depth. The concern here is with production, and emphasis will be given to the first group of constraints analyzed - blocked access to resources related to the process of production. Four issues will be analyzed: labour and managerial capacity, equipment and credit. Thus, this book does not aim at analysing all possible growth constraints. It is here suggested that the remaining constraints may constitute possible areas for further research.

Lipsey notes the importance of equipment and labour and managerial capacity in the process of production. These are factors of production, defined as the resources of a society used directly in the process of production. Without them, production cannot take place (Lipsey, 1971). Credit, in turn, supports the process of production. It has a pivotal role in the process of capitalization of the unit of production by, as already noted, keeping the circuit of capital accumulation steady. The fifth factor included in this group of constraints, lack of access to materials, will not be analyzed as a major topic. There indeed exist financial constraints related to building materials, which will be considered in the analysis of credit. However, they are not as significant as other issues because the contract builders do not deal with materials, which are bought separately by the clients.

Having defined the growth constraints, what happens when policies aimed at removing them are implemented?

The implementation of enabling policies: a move along the continuum towards capitalist production

In Chapter 1, the arguments of the liberal neo-classical and the appropriate technology approaches in favour of small-scale production of low-cost housing were put forward. They suggest a set of policy proposals to improve the capacity of small-scale builders to provide shelter in low-income settlements. However, by and large these policy proposals focus on factors which constrain the growth and capitalization of the small-scale builders, analyzed before.

As already shown, this book follows the idea that petty-commodity units of production are profit-oriented, and will move along the continuum towards capitalist production if their growth constraints are removed. Considering this, if policies in support of petty-commodity builders are implemented, their growth constraints are removed. This allows them to capitalize. However, as analyzed before, characteristics which differentiate petty-commodity from capitalist producers enable the former to produce low-cost housing in developing countries, under the present circumstances of demand in the private market. Hence, it follows that in the process of capitalization, the units lose this capacity. The above argument is supported by Gilbert, who suggests that

insofar as capital enters the low-income housing sector for purposes of land speculation, it will raise the cost of housing for the poor... Similarly, the purchase of buildings for rent, the provision of industrialised building materials, the formal provision of credit and the extension of legality to the petty-commodity production sector are likely to have the same effect. (Gilbert, 1986, p. 180).

Gilbert focuses on only some constraints. It is here suggested that his assertion also can be expanded to the other constraints examined before.

Earlier in this chapter the correlation between petty-commodity and capitalist forms of production, on the one hand, and different labour processes, on the other, was put forward. Emphasis was given to the fact that a move from petty-commodity to capitalist production entails a move at the level of the labour process. Now, another factor has been added to this scheme, i.e. the product itself. The move above described also entails a corresponding move from the production of low-cost housing to the production of other types of buildings. This process is summarized in Table 2.2.

Table 2.2
Conceptual model of the continuum of production including form of production, labour process and product

labour	PCP	Handicraft
process	CP	Elementary manufacture
	ACP	Advanced manufacture, machinofacture and post-fordism
product	PCP	Low-cost housing
	CP and ACP	Other types of buildings

Key:

PCP - petty-commodity production
CP - capitalist production
ACP - advanced capitalist production

This book takes the view that the removal of the aforementioned constraints open up possibilities for the growth of the builders. This does not mean that petty-commodity production will be extinguished, for the lacunae left empty by the builders which moved may be filled again by newcomers. This view is supported by Bernstein, Gibson and Neocosmos, who suggest that a distinction must be made between the 'fate of individual petty-commodity producers', which is to be transformed, and the 'fate of petty-commodity production in society' (Gibson and Neocosmos, 1985, p. 178), which is to be replicated constantly afresh (see also Bernstein, 1988).

However, the support given to the petty-commodity builders will, in the end, be used outside low-cost housing production. The incoming petty-commodity producers are starting afresh. If also supported, they will, *ceteris paribus*, restart the process and move. Therefore, the idea is that, although the aforementioned policies entail a dynamic process at the level of the units of production, petty-commodity production as a whole remains constant. It is not disappearing, but it is not expanding nor being strengthened. Accordingly, the role of petty-commodity production in low-cost housing does not improve.

The support given to petty-commodity builders may strengthen the building industry as a whole, which thus ends up with more equipment, credit and managerial and labour force capacity, and the like. However, considering that this reinforces the present structure of capitalist production within the industry - by opening up possibilities for capitalization of petty-commodity builders - it will not improve the supply of low-cost housing.

As already noted, the assertion about the changes in petty-commodity production and the provision of low-cost housing in developing countries entails a *ceteris paribus* clause. This clause, in turn, entails that the structure of housing supply by capitalist units of production remains unchanged. In this context, the way these units operate is not appropriate to meet the current characteristics of the demand for low-cost housing.

Obviously, if the structure of production of the capitalist units changes, the whole reasoning has to be modified. In fact, one of the suggestions put forward in this book to increase the supply of low-cost housing in developing countries is exactly the implementation of policies which alter this structure. Other suggestions include transformation of the structure of demand, and support for the development of petty-commodity builders along post-fordist lines as examined in a previous section. These suggestions will be resumed in the final chapter.

Conclusion

In order to address the questions posed in the introduction of the book, a theoretical framework was constructed in this chapter. This framework, in turn, gives origin to two sets of tentative answers to these questions.

Firstly, in relation to the factors which enable petty-commodity builders to produce low-cost housing, flexibility and prices of services have been identified as having a pivotal importance. In other words, the fact that petty-commodity builders provide services with the degree of flexibility necessary to deliver small volumes of diversified and discontinuous outputs, at a price which meets the atomized disbursements of low-income people, enable them to produce low-cost housing in developing countries.

Secondly, in relation to the process of growth of small-scale builders, out of a number of growth constraints, four have been selected to be further analyzed. Thus, petty-commodity builders face constraints related to blocked access to managerial capacity, labour capacity, equipment and credit which prevent them from capitalizing. The elimination of these constraints and the consequent movement of the builders along the continuum towards capitalist production implies their loss of the capacity to produce low-cost housing in developing countries.

The factors which enable the builders to produce low-cost housing will be elaborated in Chapter 3, followed by the growth constraints and the effects of their removal (Chapters 4 and 5).

3 Factors which enable small-scale builders to produce low-cost housing in developing countries

One of the two basic questions which this book poses is the following: *why are petty-commodity builders capable of producing low-cost housing in developing countries?* Based on the analysis developed in the previous chapter, this question is expanded here, and gives rise to the following query: *why are petty-commodity builders capable of providing services with the degree of flexibility and price necessary to satisfy the demand for low-cost housing in developing countries?* The present chapter aims at addressing this question. The labour process of petty-commodity builders is analyzed, and four factors are identified: multiple skills, simple and multi-purpose equipment, lower costs and lack of profits.

The characteristics of the labour process

The fact that petty-commodity producers are flexible in relation to capitalist ones is here understood in terms of the changes in the labour process which result from a move from petty-commodity to capitalist production. The move from handicraft to manufacture entails the introduction of a division of labour within the work process. In handicraft, a whole product is made by one person alone or together with a few apprentices and/or journeymen, using simple, multi-purpose tools. In manufacture, each producer - now a labourer - has a specific function. A given article passes through the hands of different specialized producers on its way to completion (e.g. Fundação João Pinheiro, 1984; Liberaki, 1988; Marx, 1977).

Production becomes rationalized, as it can benefit from economies of scale and increased productivity. The advantage of manufacture over handicraft is related to the economies in the means of production (e.g. buildings, store houses), and to the fact that the different stages of production which were successive can now be carried out simultaneously and continuously in terms of space, thus allowing a larger number of complete standardized goods to be produced in the same period of time. However, production becomes less flexible, because now a whole apparatus has been set up to produce a given commodity: specific tools, labourers with specific skills, particular facilities to accommodate a distinctive production process. With this structure, it is much more difficult to shift from the production of one type of commodity to another.

In the building industry, the loss of flexibility due to the need for facilities to accommodate production is minimized, compared with the manufacturing industry. Although building components are produced in factories, each product - i.e. a building - is assembled on a different site. Therefore, labourers, equipment and materials are transported to the construction site, instead of being used on specially designed structures to house in-doors production (setting aside cases such as mobile buildings). Nevertheless, due to the use of specialized skills and equipment, flexibility is also compromised in this industry in the transition from handicraft to manufacture.

The relationship between skills and flexibility - in the building industry and elsewhere - needs further clarification. The unit of production using manufacture requires the same variety of skills as a handicraft unit. However, the allocation of each specific skill to a specialized labourer, and the establishment of particular connections between each one in the production process, makes the unit as a whole more rigid. In handicraft units, skills are concentrated in the craft master, no matter whether s/he has assistants or not. Therefore, if a change in skills is required in order to cater for a change in demand, this will depend mostly on him/her. In units using manufacture, however, each skill is used by a specialized labourer at a specific point in the production process. Thus, if any change is necessary, it will require a reorganization of the connections between different labourers, and a reorganization of the production site.

The transition from handicraft to manufacture entails a transition from general-purpose tools to specialist ones (e.g. Liberaki, 1988). This transition involves a decrease in the degree of flexibility of the equipment. The introduction of machines (which are instruments able to set up the pace of production, instead of being controlled by the labourers) and the advent of machinofacture increased the productivity of the process, it further decreased the degree of flexibility of the equipment, and increased the rigidity of the process as a whole. Now the shift from the production of one commodity to another has also to deal with the replacement of heavy machines. The larger the size of the machines and/or their number in a given unit of production, the less flexible the unit becomes (e.g. Liberaki, 1988; Piore and Sabel, 1984).

The above shifts are qualitative, and refer to different products and/or different stages of production. However, flexibility also has a quantitative dimension, which is the capacity to deliver varying volumes of a given product. A petty-commodity production unit is able to deliver a small volume of goods, and can increase its output through cooperation with other units and/or subcontracting. Capitalist units are also able to increase the volume of production, and subcontracting is a widespread practice throughout the construction industry (e.g. Ball, 1988a; Grandi, 1985; Tuckman, 1983; among others). However, they cannot decrease their volume of production to the same extent as petty-commodity units, without increasing the price per unit of output. As shown in Chapter 2, low-cost housing in developing countries is built in separate stages, thus requiring units of production able to produce a limited output.

The advantages of the ability to produce a limited output have been supported by the petty-commodity production theory, by a comparison with capitalist units: as noted

36

before, petty-commodity producers survive in small-scale, risky and uncertain markets, in which capitalist producers cannot take advantage of mass-production and economies of scale (e.g. Bienefeld, 1979; Johnstone, 1984; Le Brun and Gerry, 1975; Scott, 1979). However, as noted in Chapter 2, greater flexibility alone does not enable the unit of production to provide low-cost housing. It needs the flexibility to be able to produce services at a *determinate level of prices*. This fact is explained through an analysis of prices for services provided by builders. According to economic theory, the price of a product or service is determined by the costs of production and profits (e.g. Lipsey, 1971).

The costs of production are divided into fixed and variable costs. The former costs do not change according to the level of output. The latter costs increase or decrease according to the rise and fall in level of output (Lipsey, 1971). The basic advantage of economies of scale is that they reduce costs per unit of output. Fixed costs, such as office apparatus and taxes, will decrease per unit of output, as the total volume of output rises (up to a certain threshold, when the fixed-cost element has to be increased again). Thus, the more the unit produces, the cheaper the product, assuming that output rises faster or at the same pace as the marginal variable costs (because, if costs rise faster than output, an increase in production would mean a decrease in revenue). Variable costs, although increasing in aggregate as total output rises, will also decrease per unit of output. For instance, economies regarding labour and materials can be made as production grows, by refining the division of labour within the production process, which will in turn lead to an increase in productivity.

It has been shown that capitalist units, whose labour process is based on manufacture and/or machinofacture, are able to take advantage of economies of scale, as compared with petty-commodity units of production. Thus, if production is large-scale, the capitalist will, *ceteris paribus*, have lower costs of production per unit of output. However, capitalist units are unable to benefit from economies of scale with regard to low-cost housing production in developing countries due to the specific characteristics of the demand. In the same way that fixed costs per unit of output decrease as the total volume of output rises, the reverse is also true. Thus, when lower level of output is required, as in the low-cost housing market, unitarian fixed costs will be greater.

Under these conditions, it is not possible to economize on variable costs. A relevant illustration of this fact with regard to low-cost housing production in developing countries is that rationalized processes of production are not employed. As IPT points out, rationalization aims at minimizing wastage of time, equipment and materials in the building process. This strategy is effected by improving the articulation between different stages of the building process, and the organization of the building site (IPT, 1988). However, the fact that low-income people require housing to be produced in small and discontinuous stages jeopardizes this articulation. Also, in this situation, the building site cannot be organized with a view to the construction as a whole. It has to be organized at the beginning and dismantled at the end of each stage. Thus, as the volume of production diminishes, the advantages of the capitalist process of production dwindle.

Petty-commodity building units have lower fixed costs than capitalist ones in producing the specific type of housing in question. For example, they do not have extra-production expenses such as office apparatus; and, due to the small nature of their operations, they are able to escape both regulation and the payment of taxes, as shown in Chapters 1 and 2. Thus, if the variable costs of production per unit of output are the same both for petty-commodity and for capitalist units of production, the former will have lower total costs for producing a lower level of output. Obviously, if variable costs are also lower, the petty-commodity producers have a further advantage. This is often the case. For instance, petty-commodity producers usually pay only a net sum for the work carried out by their labour force, whereas capitalist units have to pay social security taxes, and comply with minimum wage laws.

The other issue which affects the price of production of low-cost housing is profits. If there is a difference in the level of profit made by capitalist and petty-commodity producers, this will be reflected in the final price of their products. Scott and Stretton suggest that petty-commodity producers survive in markets where profit margins are low (Scott, 1979; Stretton, 1978). Since they are prepared to accept a level of profit that capitalist units would refuse to consider, it is thus implied that there are different levels of profit in different sectors of the market. The notion of a difference in the profits of capitalist and petty-commodity producers requires further elaboration. However, it is first necessary to explain the theory of equalization of profits.

Both neoclassical and Marxist economic theory recognize that competition tends to equalize rates of profit throughout the diverse areas of the capitalist economy. Capital always moves to the sectors where rates are higher, thus reducing competition in sectors where the rates are low. This fact allows the rate to rise in the latter sectors. At the same time, competition will increase in the sectors in which the rate is high, thus forcing a resultant decrease in profits (e.g. Foley, 1986). Nevertheless, equalization of profits may be prevented by a number of factors, which hinder the free movement of capital, such as differences in technology and availability of resources. This may explain the existence of lower profits in markets for products such as low-cost housing. The characteristics of this market prevent the full equalization of profits, thus hindering the penetration of capitalism, and allowing the survival of petty-commodity producers. However, a clarification of this theory is required.

The failure of capitalist producers to penetrate the low-cost housing market would, at first glance, lead to the conclusion that profit levels for petty-commodity producers would be higher due to the existence of less competition. However, in fact, profit levels are limited by the clients themselves, who are prepared to build their own houses if the price for the services of builders rises above a certain limit. This limit depends on the rate of income of the client in comparison with that of the builder (Bonduki and Rolnick, 1979; Burgess, 1992). If a low-income client is able to earn more than the cost of a builder, s/he will be better off going to work and hiring someone else to build the house. If s/he earns less, s/he may carry out the construction her/himself. In many cases, a low-income client might hire a builder even if s/he earns less than the cost of hiring him; depending on her/his expectations in terms of building standards, and technical capacity to achieve them. However, even in this case, there is a strong limitation on what a builder can charge, due to the budget constraints of the poor.

A capitalist producer would charge a profit on top of the costs of production. A petty-commodity producer, by contrast, would only charge the costs of production: i.e.

his expenses in terms of tools, transportation, apprentices and the like, plus his commission (the commission reflects the cost of his own labour, not profit as such).

To summarize, the costs of production and profits of capitalist units do not enable them to provide services at a price which meets the budgetary constrains of low-income people in developing countries. As already shown, these people can only disburse small sums of money at each stage of the construction process, and there must be a separation between one stage and the next. The prices of the services provided by the petty-commodity builders can be met by such small sums of money, since they reflect lower costs, and do not embody profit. At this level, capitalist producers are unable to economise on variable costs through the division of labour and rationalization of the production process. At the same time, they incorporate profit and higher fixed costs of production in the prices for their services. Thus, under these particular circumstances, it is more advantageous for a low-income dweller to hire a petty-commodity producer.

The factors which allow petty-commodity builders to produce low-cost housing in developing countries have been shown. The above reasoning is substantiated by empirical findings from the activities of builders working in Belo Horizonte, Brazil.

Belo Horizonte

Belo Horizonte is the capital of the Brazilian southeastern state of Minas Gerais, and is situated in a valley 858 meters above the sea level, on a transitional position between a tropical forest, stretching towards the sea, and the 'sertão', an arid zone covering a large part of the hinterland (Almanaque Abril, 1985; IBGE, 1983). The city was planned and built in the 1890s. It progressed slowly in the initial decades, but from the 1920s onwards experienced a huge process of growth, which outstripped all the forecasts of its original plan. In 1920, the population was 55,563, and grew to 600,000 in 1958, 1,781,924 in 1980 and 2,060,804 in 1993. The population of the metropolitan region in 1993 was 3,565,732 (Almanaque Abril, 1985, 1995). Similarly to many cities throughout the developing world, the growth of Belo Horizonte has been accompanied by increasing urban problems. Poverty abounds, and it is estimated that there are some 200 squatter settlements ('favelas') in the city.

The builders

Two sets of builders were interviewed in Belo Horizonte: those working (full-time or part-time) in low-cost housing production, and those not working in low-cost housing production. The former set is divided in three groups. For the purpose of this book these groups are called exclusive, mixed and hybrid builders. The latter set is divided into four groups, here called transitional, semi-capitalist, capitalist and advanced capitalist builders. The division of the builders in sets and groups is summarized in Tables 3.1 and 3.2. As the tables illustrate, the only 'pure' petty-commodity builders are in the exclusive, mixed and transitional groups (i.e. whose sole labour process is handicraft and whose sole form of production is petty-commodity). The 'pure' capitalist builders are in the capitalist and advanced capitalist groups. The remaining groups (hybrid, transitional and semi-capitalist) are in intermediary positions. For the sake of confidentiality, this book does not use the true names of the builders.

Table 3.1
The groups of builders working (full-time or part-time) in low-cost housing production, according to form of production, labour process and type of building produced

Group: Exclusive

Builders	Alberto, Amin, Evandro, João Pedro, Juvenal and Ronan
Form of production	Petty-commodity
Labour process	Artisanal
Type of building produced	Low-cost housing

Group: Mixed

Builders	Dorcelino and Tomas
Form of production	Petty-commodity
Labour process	Artisanal
Type of building produced	Low-cost housing and repair and maintenance of middle-/high-cost housing

Group: Hybrid

Builders	Augusto, Baltazar, Rafael and Waldemar
Form of production	Petty-commodity and petty-capitalist
Labour process	Artisanal and manufacture
Type of building produced	Low-cost housing and repair and maintenance and complete construction of middle-/high-cost housing

The interviews were carried out in Portuguese, which is the mother tongue of the interviewees. All the quotations extracted from them and presented in this book have been translated into English by the author. It is impossible to make a translation, no matter how accurate, without somehow modifying the original. The statements of the builders are in working-class jargon, full of slang, expressions, and grammar mistakes. However, some of these vernacular peculiarities were lost in the translation. The primary objective of the translation was to convey the contents of the verbatim reports, rather than to find precise English words or expressions adjusted to the specific original jargon.

Table 3.2

The groups of builders not working in low-cost housing production, according to form of production, labour process and type of building produced

Group: Transitional

Builder	Elisio
Form of production	Petty-commodity
Labour process	Artisanal
Type of building produced	Repair and maintenance of middle-/high-cost housing

Group: Semi-capitalist

Builder	Joaquim
Form of production	Petty-commodity and petty-capitalist
Labour process	Artisanal and manufacture
Type of building produced	Repair and maintenance and complete construction of middle-/high-cost housing

Group: Capitalist

Builders	José and Wander
Form of production	Capitalist
Labour process	Manufacture
Type of building produced	Complete construction of housing and other types of buildings for the middle- and high-income markets

Group: Advanced capitalist

Builders	Ferdinando, Gastão, Gustavo and Zelmar
Form of production	Capitalist
Labour process	Manufacture and machinofacture
Type of building produced	Complete construction of housing and other types of buildings for the middle- and high-income markets

The field work was carried out in the early 1990s, when the Brazilian currency was 'Cruzeiro' (Cr$). All prices mentioned in this book are in this currency, and the rate to the American Dollar is Cr$40.00=US$1.00.

The findings about the characteristics of the builders will be presented next.

Diversity, discontinuity and small-scale production

The exclusive builder Alberto gave the following statement about his activities:

> As you see, I am now doing the floor of this room [an extra room in a two bedroom house in the Ouro Preto neighbourhood] for Mr. Bilu. But I have

done several other things... For example, I was previously engaged in painting Mr. Mane's house, which I built two years ago... Before that, I changed the doors and windows for Mr. Bilu, and I also did bits-and-pieces for him at other times... At the end of last year I did the concrete work for the house of the Zaira family - you know, that family just has money to build one floor, but they plan to build a second one some day and rent or sell it to make some money. I built the frame for the house, pillars, beams and the roof, ready for a second floor later on. When I finish my present job, I will go back to the Zaira's to build the walls.

The capacity of the exclusive builders to provide small-scale services is illustrated by their account of the minimum tasks which they were prepared to undertake: 'fix one door or window' (Alberto, Amin and Evandro); 'change the floor of a kitchen' (João Pedro); 'change the floor of a bathroom' (Juvenal); 'fix a door' (Ronan).

The mixed builders, second group engaged in low-cost housing production, work in low-income settlements similarly to the exclusive builders. As Tomas illustrates:

> My present job is fixing a tile roof for the Pachecos... Before that, I built the walls and fixed the asbestos roof of another house... Before that, I did the flooring of yet another house, for Mr. Laercio... And before Mr. Laercio, I built the walls for the Pachecos, the family for whom I am now working again... After finishing my present job, I will do some plumbing work - one bathroom, kitchen and laundry area - for the Pereiras... The Pereiras hired me to build their house last year; but, after the roofing, they stopped construction due to financial constraints.

The mixed builders also undertake repair and maintenance work for middle- and high-income families. With regard to these activities, Tomas said the following:

> The same flexibility that I need to work in low-income settlements I need to do repairs for the rich. It is one door here today, a tap there tomorrow, a light bulb the day after... But I prefer to carry out these activities, you know, because they are better paid than those in low-income settlements.

Thus, the mixed builders need flexibility to carry out their activities inside and outside low-income settlements. The fact that they prefer to work outside will be analyzed later.

The third group of builders engaged in low-cost housing production are the hybrids. Their activities in low-income settlements are similar to those of the exclusive and mixed builders. A general account of the situation was given by Augusto:

> You could describe my work in low-income neighbourhoods perhaps as that of an acrobat!... I have always to keep changing activities here... Each day that I work here, when I wake up I think: oh, God, would it be possible to work today smoothly, or will there be another problem?... Will the client tell me that he could not get the material, or that I should stop because he does

not have money to pay me?... Or will he change the plan of the house yet again in order to adapt to new cheap materials that he has bought?

The ability of the hybrid and mixed builders to provide small-scale services is evidenced by the minimum tasks which they were ready to accept: 'even fix a tap' (Baltazar); 'even fix one leakage on a roof' (Rafael); 'fix a tap, or a plug' (Augusto); 'fix the installations in a bathroom' (Waldemar); 'fix one door or window' (Dorcelino); 'plumbing work on a bathroom' (Tomas).

The hybrid builders also build complete residences for middle- and high-income families. The dilemma that these builders face, alternating between the artisanal production of low-cost housing and the manufactured production of middle- and high-cost housing, is illustrated by the following testimony given by Rafael:

> I prefer to build complete houses. When I get a contract, I sit down, plan the whole work carefully, and start the job... I earn more than in scattered jobs in low-income settlements; and, besides, I have security of work for several months... Unfortunately, I do not have enough demand to allow me to build complete houses continuously... After finishing one house, I dismantle the production scheme, and go back to scattered activities until I get another full house contract... When I finish the construction of a complete house, I cannot maintain my production plan and use it in the dispersed contracts given to me in low-income neighbourhoods... In the construction of a complete house, there is a close link between the different phases of construction. The site is organized for the whole production, there is no distance between different phases, because they are all part of the same construction... But I lose this in a low-income neighbourhood... How can I link the construction of one foundation in one house here, with the construction of the walls of another house which is far away from it, and the roof of a third one?... They are different, disconnected sites... And the workforce, though? If I have six labourers working together, under my supervision, in the construction of a complete house, fine. But it is not the same thing having them scattered across six different jobs in six different sites in low-income neighbourhoods... They do not combine their work, produce less, and instead of supervising them at the same time, I have to do it one by one... Besides all that, there is the problem of the frequent stoppage of work in poor neighbourhoods, due to the economic difficulties of the people... It makes it impossible to plan my activities thoroughly, but I have to plan if I have a group of workers with me.

Thus, as the case of Rafael shows, hybrid builders lose the ability to build low-cost housing when they set up a scheme of production based on a manufactured labour process. The problems of manufacture with reference to construction in low-income settlements will be elaborated later, through the examination of the cases of builders which do not produce low-cost housing.

The cases of the groups of builders who produce low-cost housing have been presented now. The major findings are the following:

. All three groups of builders are capable of providing services with the degree of flexibility necessary to produce small volumes of a diversified and discontinuous output, thus attending the demand for low-cost housing.

. Mixed builders also use their flexibility to carry out repair and maintenance work outside low-income settlements. They prefer to carry out these activities rather than to build low-cost housing. This finding will be used later to explain the process of growth of builders.

. Hybrid builders prefer to build complete middle- and high-cost residences. However, during the period in which they are engaged in these activities, they use a labour process which prevents them from producing low-cost housing. This finding will also be used to explain the process of growth of builders.

In order to examine the characteristics of builders who produce low-cost housing from a broader perspective, attention will be given to builders who were only engaged in construction outside low-income settlements. As noted before, they are divided in four groups: transitional, semi-capitalist, capitalist and advanced capitalist.

The transitional builder Elisio undertakes repair and maintenance work for middle- and high-income families, using an artisanal process. His present activities are similar to those demanded in low-income settlements:

> One who works in repair and maintenance has to be prepared to carry out a large number of diverse activities; a pattern-activity does not exist... I do everything, no matter the scale: fixing a shower, a lock in a door, a broken tile, everything.

Therefore, Elisio, who is a petty-commodity builder, has the flexibility to provide diverse, discontinuous and small-scale services. However, he does not produce low-cost housing any more. This is due to the price of his services, which will be analyzed later on.

The case of the semi-capitalist builder is different. Joaquim now caters for the middle-class market. He uses handicraft and a manufactured labour process, doing everything from repair and maintenance to construction of complete residences:

> I would prefer to carry on building complete residences. I earn more... But when I cannot do it, I go to small jobs, in many cases for families for whom I have built a house before, or their friends... They can afford what I charge for my services, whereas the poor cannot.

Thus, like the hybrid builders, the semi-capitalist builder is unable to produce low-cost housing by using a manufacture process like that used to construct complete residences. Even when using an artisanal labour process, he charges a price for his services which the low-income people cannot pay.

The capitalist builders, in turn, use a manufactured process and produce complete residences for middle- and high-income people on a full-time basis. José, for instance, said the following:

The volume of my output varies. Sometimes I work with only a few labourers in the construction of individual houses, at others I build more than one house at the same time... But I will not take a contract which is smaller than a 50 square meters house.

Thus, José has the flexibility necessary to produce a diverse output, but his minimum output is much larger than that required by low-income people. In terms of the discontinuity of production, he stated the following:

Even if I am building one house at a time, I try my best to begin the construction of each house immediately after the finishing of the previous one... Interruptions are harmful to me. If there is a gap between the construction of a new house and that of the previous one, I have to pay the wages of the men while they are doing nothing... But if I dismiss them, I have to pay redundancy fines, and, in order to begin a new construction, I have to spend money on recruiting.

The final group of builders studied, who work only outside low-income settlements, is the advanced capitalist. They use a process which is a mixture of manufacture and machinofacture, and produce on a larger scale than the previous groups. Gastão, for instance, describes his activities as follows:

I build series of similar houses and flats... A minimum of four to six and a maximum of ten to twelve houses at any one time, or one apartment block at a time... Each apartment block has a minimum of six flats and a maximum of twenty.

Gastão's minimum output is larger than that of all the builders previously examined. He also compares his work with those in low-cost housing production:

I know that I cannot build low-cost housing using my present scheme of production. How can I use this scheme in the low-income areas? I cannot build beforehand to sell later, because the poor do not have the means to pay... I have to build to order, and the houses are all different from each other... In such circumstances, I cannot rationalize production, which is essential to increase my profits.

Gustavo, Zelmar and Ferdinando are the other builders in the advanced capitalist group. Gustavo, like Gastão, is a speculative builder. He also acknowledges that his present labour process does not allow him to penetrate the low-cost housing market. Zelmar and Ferdinando are contract builders (thus building one house at a time), but do not cater for the poor either. They both have a certain level of flexibility enabling them to produce different buildings, using different systems of construction. However, Zelmar has declared that a minimum contract would, for him, be a single high-income residence of approximately 300 square meters. For Ferdinando, the minimum is a single high-income residence, or a three storey apartment block. Neither of these two builders is capable of building a house in discontinuous stages.

The cases of all the builders examined have now been set out. They confirm the postulate that petty-commodity builders have the flexibility to deliver small volumes of a diversified and discontinuous output, thus catering for the demand for low-cost housing. The findings about the capitalist and advanced capitalist builders show that this flexibility is exclusive to petty-commodity builders. The advanced capitalists Gastão and Gustavo do not produce a diverse, discontinuous or small-scale output. The capitalist builders, together with the other two advanced capitalist builders, produce various types of building, but neither discontinuously nor on a small-scale. These findings confirm the existence of a continuum running from petty-commodity to capitalist production, as suggested in Chapter 2. The case studies also reveal the existence of transient cases, i.e. the mixed, hybrid, transitional and semi-capitalist builders. This reiterates the aforementioned continuum.

Prices for services

Among the builders who produce low-cost housing, the exclusive builder Alberto gives the following account of the prices for his services:

> The price for my services is based on the number of days that a contract takes. When I start a contract, I estimate how long it will take me to execute it... I am only charging Cr$350.00 a day. But this is the work which I can get for the moment... I do not have contacts with the rich enabling me to work for them, and I have not found another job yet... Cr$350.00 is just for my services. If I need an apprentice or a journeyman to help me, I charge the client separately... It is Cr$150.00 per day for the apprentice, and around Cr$250.00 for the journeyman... The price of the building materials is completely separate from the price of my services... I just help the client to calculate the materials which will be necessary, and he pays the suppliers directly.

Alberto's method of pricing has been confirmed by all the other builders who produce low-cost housing. The daily rates of these builders range from Cr$350.00 to Cr$600.00 to produce low-cost housing. The rate for apprentices varies from Cr$100.00 to Cr$250.00 per day, and for journeymen, from Cr$200.00 to Cr$300.00.

Low-income clients usually spread the costs of labour and materials over different periods of time, in order to afford to pay for the construction. Considering the rates that the builders charge for their own work, and what they pay for their workforce, the expenditure of a client when hiring one low-cost housing builder, two apprentices and one journeyman for one week varies from Cr$5,400.00 to Cr$7,800.00. This proved to be affordable by their low-income clients. However, the situation regarding the other builders examined in this book is different.

The rates of builders only working outside low-income settlements will now be presented. The transitional builder Elisio charges Cr$1,100.00 per day for his work.

He pays Cr$250.00 and Cr$350.00 for his apprentices and journeymen respectively. The criterion for his fees is as follows:

> You know, most independent builders like me were labourers in big companies before... So, we base our prices according to what a labourer earns... We want to gain more working as a builder; otherwise, it is better to go back to work as a labourer... The rate for an 8 hour-day of work for a registered labourer in the building industry is now from Cr$360.00 to Cr$600.00, depending on the craft and the company... So, I want more than that.

The semi-capitalist builder Joaquim adopts the same criterion as a basis for his fees. Both Elisio and Joaquim charge twice as much the maximum rate of the builders who work in low-income settlements.

The capitalist builders Wander and José and the advanced capitalist builders Zelmar and Ferdinando charge for their services in a different way. Wander declared that:

> I build full houses... So, I calculate all the costs of construction, and the client pays me weekly... My minimum output is an entire house... I do not build more than that - that is, if a client wants to pay me the price of an entire house, I go and build even just one wall... But of course no one is going to hire me for that... The price of the minimum house I built, converted at today's rate is Cr$1,455,043.00, excluding land... We can consider that as the minimum I am prepared to build.

Wander's minimum implies a weekly disbursement of Cr$84,877.57, which is obviously impossible for a low-income family, whose maximum monthly income would be around Cr$10,140.00 (i.e. the equivalent to three official minimum wages). Household income is used by Brazilian agencies as an index to define poverty. Poor households are those whose income is below three times the regional minimum wage established by the Brazilian government (e.g. Almanaque Abril, 1985).

The case of José is similar to that of Elisio in terms of minimum output and price range. The case of Zelmar is the following:

> My minimum output is a single residence of approximately 300 square meters... I can build it for Cr$8,124,480.00, excluding land... You know, in contract building the client pays us weekly... So, a client would have to pay an average of Cr$156,240.00 per week to build this house.

Ferdinando charges in the same way. His minimum output is a single high-income residence, or a three-storey block of six middle-quality pattern flats, of approximately 100 square meters each. The cost of each flat is Cr$2,228,353.20, which is cheaper than a house. In a system of condominium, a client has to pay Cr$42,852.95 per week on average for a flat. Gastão, in turn, has shown that his cheapest housing unit costs Cr$1,648,432.50. The case of Gustavo is similar. He also sells flats in the same price range. So, in order to buy a residence built by one of them, a family would need to disburse a sum correspondent to its full price - Cr$1,648,432.50 for the cheapest housing unit.

Thus, in conclusion, the proposition that petty-commodity builders provide services for a price which meets the atomized disbursements of the low-income people is confirmed. The mixed and hybrid builders are found to be in a transitory position in the process of capitalization. They produce low-cost housing, but also cater for middle- and high-income families, with prices which are inappropriate to the low-income market. Transitional and semi-capitalist builders also provide services for which the poor can pay. However, as they charge more than the exclusive, mixed and hybrid producers, they provide less for the same amount of money, and are therefore not hired by low-income clients. They too are in a transitory position as regards the process of capitalization. The price of the capitalist and advanced capitalist builders is definitely beyond the reach of low-income people.

Therefore, by combining the findings about flexibility and prices, it is shown that a low-income client is able to hire a petty-commodity builder for a very short period of time to carry out a specific small-scale task, if s/he does not have the means to afford a longer contract. This scheme allows a client to build her/his house in stages. The opportunity to make a phased investment in construction and to halt the process whenever necessary is more valuable than a lower price for the whole construction, considering that the latter implies constant disbursements. However, why do the petty-commodity builders have the attributes analyzed above?

Characteristics of the builders

The aim of this section is to demonstrate that multiple skills, simple and general-purpose equipment, lower costs of production and a lack of profit are factors which enable petty-commodity builders to have the degree of flexibility and prices necessary to cater for the demand for low-cost housing.

Skills

The first group of builders who produce low-cost housing is the exclusive. Alberto, Amin, Ronan and Juvenal started their careers as bricklayers in registered building units, and Evandro as a reinforcement fixer. Juvenal later increased his specialization by concentrating only on finishing. These five builders eventually left their jobs to work independently in low-cost housing production. In order to carry out this activity, they had to diversify and learn other skills through a process of direct observation and on-the-job training. João Pedro started working with his father (also a builder), and with him learned all the skills necessary to build low-cost housing.

The two mixed builders (Dorcelino and Tomas) and one hybrid builder (Baltazar) started with one particular craft and expanded their skills progressively, like most of the exclusive builders. The remaining hybrid builders (Augusto, Rafael and Waldemar) learned all their skills with their fathers.

At any rate, despite of having different starting points, the aforementioned builders had to learn multiple skills to build low-cost housing. In the words of Tomas:

48

I began as a bricklayer-trainee in the Arcgel [a registered construction firm]... After being upgraded, I specialized in finishing. But then I quit the firm and went to the Santa Terezinha neighbourhood, where there was a lot of work for independent builders... But, on many occasions, I started building for a given client, and then had to stop without notice because he has suddenly run out of money... If that happens I have to pick up any casual activity that is available, until the client calls me back or until I find something else... This has been a regular occurrence... For me, a large amount of one type of work corresponds to a small amount of various types of work... But a large amount of one type of work does not exist there... I had to expand my skills to increase my chances... Nowadays I know everything necessary to build a house in this [low-income] area... So, no matter what part of the house the client wants to build, I can help him.

However, the construction of complete residences outside low-income settlements is different. As Rafael puts it:

Here [in low-income settlements] you see the way I work... A jack of all trades... But the construction of an entire house is different... There I am only the manager, and I have to be, if I want things to go smoothly... The whole point of putting a large number of workers together is that each one does a specific task, and does it well and quickly... I don't care how many skills my workers have... How many courses, diplomas, whatever... They are paid to do one specific job... It is like a football team. Each player in his position, doing a specific thing, in order to achieve the goal... The whole construction becomes stiff, there is not much room for alterations... But this is the idea, this is how we earn.

Thus, the case of Rafael illustrates that, in order to build complete residences, hybrid builders establish a manufacture production process in which the emphasis is on specialization rather than multiplicity in terms of skills.

The cases of these builders who only work outside low-income settlements will now be discussed. The transitional and the semi-capitalist builders, Evandro and Joaquim, still have a multiplicity of skills, giving them a capacity for diverse and discontinuous production. This is essential for their present repair and maintenance activities for middle- and high-income households. However, they are no longer capable of producing low-cost housing. The factors which prevent them from doing so will be analyzed later.

The case of the capitalist and advanced capitalist builders is a distinct one. Wander, José, Gastão and Gustavo also worked in low-income settlements in the past, thus using a multiplicity of skills. However, they do not use their multiple skills any more.

The case of Wander illustrates the changes in tasks and skills which took place as his unit of production grew. His career as a construction labourer and the process of his acquisition of skills is similar to that of most of the builders analyzed before. Thus, Wander's unit of production incorporates all the diverse skills necessary to produce

49

low-cost housing. However, it does not operate in low-income settlements. Wander's explanation is the following:

> When I worked in low-income settlements, the firm was basically me; eventually one or two more people... Then I had all the skills to deal with all the different things that the poor requested of me, and to change from one task to another quickly when a problem arose... But now the firm is much beyond me... It is me plus all my workers... Although each labourer has a different skill, the firm as a whole functions only in a determined fashion... I pay my workers to carry out specific and connected functions, that is the way we can benefit... I gain from planning at least a medium-scale contract, and then executing it according to the plans... After planning, the execution becomes rigid... I cannot afford to shift constantly from producing one thing to another... This is just when me or my labourers could use diverse skills... But nowadays I gain exactly from not using diverse skills, I gain from using specialized skills.

The situations of José, Gastão and Gustavo replicate that of Wander. Ferdinando and Zelmar (advanced capitalist builders) started their units on a capitalist level, with a specialized labour force from the beginning. However, their cases also replicate those of the other capitalist and advanced capitalist builders, in relation to the inadequacy of their skills to produce low-cost housing.

To conclude, the above findings show that multiple skills give petty-commodity builders the degree of flexibility necessary to cater for the demand for low-cost housing. When using an artisanal petty-commodity production process, a builder utilizes multiple skills. When using a manufacture capitalist process, skills become specialized.

Equipment

Most of the equipment used by the builders who produce low-cost housing are simple, general-purpose tools, which could be used for different tasks. With small variations, this set of equipment is the following:

(i) Excavation: the hoe is used to mix small quantities of concrete, beside its digging functions. It is also used outside the construction industry, like the shovel, in diverse digging activities, such as gardening and farming. The digging tool is a rough metal stick, which can be used for destroying hard parts of the soil, but also for breaking any hard material, such as pieces of concrete. The auger is the most specialized equipment for excavation, and is used for digging earth. They are all very simple equipment, in terms of design and operation.

(ii) Earthwork: the rammer is also simple and multipurpose. It is used to level the floor, but can also be used to level concrete roofs and pavements.

(iii) Measuring: the tape measure is used throughout the construction process in many different ways. The wire and nylon rope are used in the same manner, and can also be used to tie goods or materials together. Wire is also used to isolate parts of the construction site which should not be entered at a given stage. The rubber hose is used not only for measuring, but also for cleaning the site and the building. These tools also have many applications outside construction. The flooring board is a very basic equipment, merely a piece of wood used to level the floor after pouring cement, but which can also be used for other purposes, such as framing for concrete. The builder's square is a very simple tool, specific for the measurement of angles, but which can be used in different stages of the construction. The spirit level is specifically designed to measure levels, but, like the square, can also be used at different stages: walls, wood frames for concreting, doors and windows. The metal level is designed to measure the vertical level of walls. These are all very simple tools.

(iv) Cutting: the saw is used for various types of wood, and the mechanical bandsaw for various types of metal. The pliers are used for cutting materials such as wire, but are also used for other tasks such as the removal of nails and screws. They are used not only in construction, but also in domestic functions. The planer is specifically intended for shovelling wood, and has a more sophisticated design as compared to the former equipment.

(v) Striking: the hammer is used in different stages for the fixing of nails, as well as to make holes and cuts in bricks and walls. The cleaver can also be used to cut bricks, walls, concrete and thinly reinforcement steel. The cleaver has to be used together with a heavy club, which is a rough hammer used to hit it, and is also used alone to break rocks or rough parts of walls as well as concrete.

(vi) Perforation: the manual drill is used specifically to make holes in wood.

(vii) Mixing of concrete: takes place on a platform, which is merely a flat piece of wood. The only equipment used in the process which has any specialized function is the mesh, which is used to sieve the sand to remove the lumps and rubbish.

(viii) Finishing: the trowel is used for putting mortar between the bricks in bricklaying, and for different types of finishing of the walls after the bricks have been set. The metal float is used to level floors and walls, as well as to spread cement and/or glue mix which fixes tiles.

(ix) Transport: the wheel-barrow and bucket are used at all different stages of the construction process, and even used outside it, for instance, in gardening or farming.

(x) Painting: brushes, a paint tray and spatula. This set of equipment is specialized but simple.

(xi) Concrete reinforcing: reinforcement fixing plate, reinforcement bar and steel shears. The first one is multi-purpose (it is also used as a basis for cutting or reshaping materials). The second and third are specialized.

(xii) Installations: wrenches are used for this purpose as well as to hold materials which need cutting and reshaping. Pliers are also used in other operations already described. Screwdrivers are also used for fixing other equipment, and for domestic purposes.

The exclusive builder Amin gives the following account about the role of his equipment in low-cost housing construction:

> With my tools I can work in a [low-income] neighbourhood like this one here because they are simple to operate... They are economical, because most

of them can be used for different functions during the construction... Some of them are tools which I need in my own house, which means economy... If I had to buy a new tool for each operation, my expenditure would be much larger... The conjunction of my skills and tools allows me to carry out many different activities... As I already told you, different activities are fundamental to cope with the variations and the uncertainties in the type of construction in these neighbourhoods here... And each tool, on its own, enables me to perform tiny operations... As I also mentioned to you, there are no large-scale operations here.

As the case of Amin illustrates, the exclusive builders have acquired simple multi-purpose tools, which have allowed them to operate on a diverse, discontinuous and small-scale basis (i.e. to produce low-cost housing). The mixed and hybrid builders have acquired this set of equipment as well. However, they also own others, necessary for their activities outside low-income settlements.

The mixed builder Tomas also has a marble cutter, a grooving plane (for cutting), a monkey wrench, threading dye (for installations) and a power drill (for perforation). The other mixed builder (Dorcelino) owns the above equipment plus a circular table power saw, a sanding machine, a power planer, a manual double saw, a grooving plane and a chisel (for carpentry). Most of these tools are specialized. In the words of Tomas:

> The low-cost houses built by me did not require the use of these tools... Poor people are much more concerned with paying a small sum of money rather than having a service done with precision and good finishing... Thus, I do not need to use tools such as marble saw, power drill, grooving plane there... The other tools are cheap... Cheap tools like a hoe, a hammer, a trowel or a saw, I don't even remember their price... and I don't charge for them when I give the price for my services... But with this equipment here, I cannot do that... They are expensive, you know... It wasn't easy for me to buy them... I either have to make my services more expensive, or use these tools enough to recuperate what I have spent... But I cannot do any of these things in the construction of low-cost housing... Thus, why waste them in low-income settlements, if they are not necessary there... I only bought them because I can use them in the south zone [middle- and high-income neighbourhoods in Belo Horizonte]... It is not worth investing in them just to build low-cost housing, they are not necessary there.

The hybrid builders also use this equipment, but still need others in order to carry out the construction of complete residences. With small variations, this extra set includes a power sander (for the finishing of wooden floors), a concrete pistol (to perforate concrete), a steel cutting machine (to cut steel for concrete reinforcement with a diameter up to 2"), pincers (to cut the wire which holds the reinforcement steel), a circular table power saw (to cut the large quantities of wood necessary for roof structures and concrete frames), bench vice (to hold firmly any material which needs to be dealt with for cutting, reshaping, etc), a handbarrow (to transport larger quantities of cement, sand and aggregates to the concrete mixer), concrete mixer (which can mix up to 2.5 cubic meters), a pneumatic drill (necessary to distribute larger quantities of concrete evenly in the frames). Most of this equipment is specialized, and not used in low-cost housing production. As Rafael and Baltazar respectively state:

> The finishing of low-income houses does not require specialized equipment... It does not require an accurate cutting and reshaping of tubes and other material, does not require a carefully made wooden floor, does not require perforation of concrete.

> I would never spend money in this equipment for concrete mixing and reinforcing if I were only working in low-income areas, where the quantity of concrete used in each contract is at a minimum... I would not need a circular table power saw, because in the construction of small houses there is no need for concrete framing or for a complex roof structure... There is no need to cut large quantities of wood... Having bought this equipment, I have to recover the money, or else I would be paying in order to work.

Several multi-purpose tools used in low-cost housing production are also used in the construction of complete residences, such as, for instance, the builder's square, trowel, wheel-barrow, flooring board, amongst others. However, several other tools are replaced. The final balance between those which are multi-purpose and those which are specialized inclines towards the latter.

The difference between the equipment used within and outside low-income settlements will be further illustrated by the cases of the builders which do not produce low-cost housing.

Elisio, the transitional builder, and Joaquim, the semi-capitalist builder, use a set of equipment similar to those used by the mixed builders interviewed, as well as specialized equipment used for finishing wooden floors and perforating concrete. Joaquim also needs other equipment described in the case of the hybrid builders, in order to carry out the construction of complete dwellings. Wander and José, the capitalist builders, use a set of equipment necessary to build complete residences for middle- and high-income families, presented in the case of the hybrid builders. They also use a van for their work, in order to deal with several construction sites at the same time. Gustavo, Gastão, Zelmar and Ferdinando, the advanced capitalist builders, use equipment equivalent to those used by the capitalist builders. However, they also use other equipment for erecting multi-storey buildings (pile hammer, scaffolding, winch, vibrating tamper, concrete mixer).

The whole set of tools necessary to build low-cost housing costs around Cr$12,500.00 in retail shops in Belo Horizonte. However, the specialized equipment is much more expensive. For example, a pile hammer alone costs Cr$210,000.00, and a concrete mixer Cr$179,000.00. As Gustavo states:

> This [specialized] equipment was very hard to buy, and there is no point in going into low-cost housing construction to leave these tools idle... It is a

two-way barrier in terms of equipment... Many of the simple tools which I used when I worked in low-income settlements, I cannot use them now... But, on the other hand, my new equipment is not good for low-cost housing production.

In short, the findings drawn from builders working outside the low-income market shows that there is a difference between their set of equipment and that used in low-cost housing production. The findings about the mixed, hybrid, transitional and semi-capitalist builders reveal that they use simple, multi-purpose equipment in low-cost housing production. However, they also use another set of equipment, which is specialized and expensive, to work in another niche of petty-commodity production: repair and maintenance for middle- and high-income households. However, as they are of no use in low-cost housing production, their acquisition constitutes an incentive for builders to engage in alternative construction activities, which increases the price of their services.

Costs of production

The costs of production of the builders who produce low-cost housing include their own fees, the occasional fees for apprentices and journeymen, and sometimes transportation. In the words of the exclusive builder Alberto:

> My expenditure on tools is insignificant, for they were cheap, and I bought them over a period of a number of years... I do not include them in my costs of production... What I charge is just my daily rate, Cr$350.00, and, if appropriate, that of my assistants... Most of my work is in this area, where I live... But if the work is far, and I have to take a bus... I have to spend Cr$10.00, Cr$20.00 per day... In this case, I haggle with the client... If he refuses, I do the work anyway, because I have to eat... In this case, then, I take home Cr$340.00 or Cr$330.00 a day, rather than Cr$350.00... But besides that, I have no other costs.

As noted before, the daily rates for the workforce for the production of low-cost housing varies between Cr$100.00 and Cr$250.00 for an apprentice and between Cr$200.00 to Cr$300.00 for a journeyman. These variations are due to the qualifications of each worker, and to the extent of his contacts to get work.

The daily rates of the builders range from Cr$350.00 to Cr$600.00 to produce low-cost housing. The level of productivity of the different builders is similar. Differences in their daily fees result mainly from the level of demand for the services of each builder.

In order to put the costs of low-cost housing production into perspective, the costs of other construction activities will be now examined. When undertaking repair and maintenance for middle- and high-income families, mixed builders are found to charge a higher fee. As Dorcelino said,

We can charge more when we work in the south zone [middle- and high-income neighbourhoods], and we do so... But we do it by reference to what the masons are charging... We want to gain more than them... Considering what I earn from this work, it was worth buying the equipment that I now have...

When building complete residences for middle- or high-income families, hybrid builders charge on a different basis from that adopted when building low-cost housing. As Augusto stated:

There are differences between the construction of an entire house, and what I do in low-income settlements... Low-cost housing is basically an illegal activity... Officially, any alteration in a building has to be previously approved by the municipal authorities; but by and large they do not bother with what is happening in low-income areas... But the case of the construction of a new house, or even the extension of an existing house in a posh zone is different... First, you cannot hide these activities... And second, you cannot sell a house which does not legally exist... Or at least its price will drop significantly... The fact that the construction of a full house is a regulated activity has implications in terms of costs... First, the plan of the house must be approved beforehand, therefore you have to pay for the design, plus the taxes for approval... Then you have the CREA taxes [to regularize the construction site]; and, later, you have to pay the 'baixa' and 'habite-se' [to allow the building to be occupied]... Moreover, I am not a qualified engineer, you know, and there has to be an engineer in charge of the construction site, otherwise the construction will be halted... This means that I have to pay a fee to an engineer to be legally responsible for the construction... He does not go to the site, you know... He just signs the paper on my behalf... I am the actual builder, but I do not have a degree, and have to pay him, and he charges around 1% of the whole cost of construction!

Apart from expenses relating to taxes and fees, there are other costs involved in the construction of a complete residence:

The equipment that I use does not amount to a large proportion of the costs of construction... It amounts to around 1.5% of each contract... But it is an expenditure anyway, isn't it?... And I have to include it... If I rent, then I transfer the cost of the rent to the client... But even if I don't rent, I transfer the cost at least of my more expensive equipment, because I had to pay for it anyway... And when it breaks I have to pay for fixing it or buy another one... There are also transport expenses. It is not just me and half a dozen tools boarding a bus any more... It is a lot of equipment and sometimes labourers. But, actually, the greatest expense is the workforce... I told you that in low-income settlements we pay cash-in-hand to the men... But in a registered construction, we have to pay their social expenses, which are 110% of the wages!

55

The costs of builders who do not produce low-cost housing are found to replicate those of mixed and hybrid builders in their activities outside low-income settlements. Elisio, the transitional builder studied, has a structure of costs similar to that required for the production of low-cost housing. However, he charges Cr$1,100.00 and pays Cr$250.00 per day for an apprentice, and Cr$350.00 for a journeyman. Therefore, his costs are higher than those of low-cost housing builders, considering that both groups share the same level of productivity. Joaquim, the semi-capitalist builder, incurs different costs for different types of work. For repair and maintenance, his costs are similar to those of Elisio. Like that builder, Joaquim charges and pays his workforce more than the low-cost housing builders studied. In the construction of complete residences, his cost structure is similar to that described in the testimony of the hybrid builder Augusto. Wander and José, the capitalist builders, have all the expenses of the semi-capitalist and hybrid builders when building complete residences. Moreover, both builders pay bookkeepers who charge an average of Cr$500.00 per hour of work to keep their accounts. The expenses of this operation are spread on the contracts which they take. Advanced capitalist builders have other costs of production, since all of them are registered building units. As Gastão puts it,

> You cannot avoid paying taxes if you have a registered firm... Plus wages for the office personnel, rent, telephone and electricity bills, photocopying, mail, and the like.

The cost structures of semi-capitalist, capitalist and advanced capitalist builders are applicable to large-scale production, and not to the production of low-cost housing. These costs thus have a negative influence on their capacity to produce a limited output. Ferdinando, for example, said:

> There are ways in which I can economize, when I erect larger buildings... One of them is on materials. First you save if you buy in large quantities, by purchasing directly from the producer rather than from the retail seller... And you also save on transportation... And materials such as, for example, tubes, reinforcement steel, electrical cables, or wood for concrete framing always come in standardized pieces, and you have to cut them to adapt to the demands of each individual building... But when you cut, you always waste some material... And because there is a minimum size for standardized pieces, you end up losing more in small-scale buildings... The larger the building, the easier it is to avoid waste... Take a piece of equipment such as scaffolding as another example. It is sold by modules, and there is also a minimum size... So, in a small building which needs this equipment, you have to buy the minimum module anyway... But in a larger building, you can utilize the same [minimum] module several times, if you want to economize... And, as I told you before, labour can also be saved by the use of some equipment, such as the concrete mixer, steel cutter machine, pneumatic drill... Labour can be used with great efficiency in a carefully planned large-scale contract... In which the several stages of a given construction are well coordinated.

Different attitudes towards the production of low-cost housing are illustrated by the following quotations. For example, the advanced capitalist builder Zelmar said:

> It is not only the total volume of activities which counts, but also the scale of each individual activity... A small number of large-scale activities is not equal to a large number of small-scale activities.

In comparison, the mixed builder Tomas claimed:

> For me, a large amount of one type of work corresponds to a small amount of various types of work.

In summary, costs of production represent one of two elements which comprise the price for the services of petty-commodity builders. Since they are low, they influence the capacity of these builders to have a degree of flexibility to deliver small outputs at a price which suits the budget constraints of low-income people. In comparison, it is shown that the cost structures of the builders who use a capitalist form of production are such that they are only advantageous when economies of scale are possible. This is found to be impossible at present in low-income settlements. The findings concerning the mixed, hybrid, transitional and semi-capitalist builders reveal that their costs are sufficiently low to enable them to produce low-cost housing. However, their costs when carrying out other construction work are found to be higher, thus confirming that they are in a state of transition in the continuum of production.

Profits

The second element which constitutes the price of the services of a builder is profits. None of the builders who produce low-cost housing charge profit in their work in low-income settlements. They charge a daily fee, which is not calculated in addition to the costs of production, but by reference to the wages currently being paid by registered units of production for labourers in the construction industry. Mixed builders charge in the same way when undertaking repair and maintenance work for middle- and high-income families.

Profits may however be made by hybrid builders working outside low-income settlements. Two of them, Waldemar and Augusto, still charge a daily fee. But Baltazar and Rafael charge profits. As Baltazar puts it:

> The rule for building a complete residence is that you calculate the costs of the construction, and put a profit on top of that... My profit is around 10% of the costs... In the costs, I include my own work as the manager of the construction process... So, managerial fees and profits are distinct from each other... That is the way the market operates.

When questioned about the way in which Augusto and Waldemar charge, Baltazar replied:

I know that there are builders who charge daily... But that is their problem... They do not charge profits, O.K., but their process of construction is less organized... The client has to be there, checking most of the time... I do not give a headache to my clients... They do not have to worry about anything.

The cases of the builders which do not produce low-cost housing will now be presented. Like the mixed builders, the transitional builder Elisio incorporates no profit element into his costs. He merely charges a daily fee. Joaquim, the semi-capitalist builder, charges a profit on the construction of complete residences, but not on repair and maintenance work. However, the capitalist and advanced capitalist builders always charge a profit. José, for instance, stipulates a minimum sum for profit, for less than which he is not willing to produce. This, together with the costs of production, limits his minimum output. As he said:

> My minimum output is a house of 50 square meters. If I produce less than that, my costs start eating my profits... I would still have to pay the taxes, the engineer, the bookkeeper, you know.

His minimum profit is around Cr$12,700.00 per week. This is more than three times the monthly minimum wage - the upper limit of the poverty line in the area. Thus, a low-income person could not afford to pay even the weekly profits of José.

In short, a lack of profit influences the capacity of builders who use a petty-commodity form of production to have a degree of flexibility to deliver a small output at a price which meets the atomized disbursements of the low-income people. In comparison, the builders who use a capitalist form of production are found to charge profits which are beyond the means of the poor. The practices of intermediate groups of builders (e.g. hybrid and semi-capitalist builders) show a variable situation. Some of these builders make a profit while others do not, and the decision whether or not to include a profit element in their fee depends on the nature of the work undertaken. This confirms their position of transition on the continuum of production, previously mentioned.

Conclusion

At the beginning of this chapter, a question was asked as to the factors which enable petty-commodity builders to produce low-cost housing in developing countries. A set of findings was presented to shown that petty-commodity builders cater for the demand for low-cost housing by providing services with a degree of flexibility necessary to deliver small volumes of a diversified and discontinuous output and with a price which meets the atomized disbursements of the low-income people. Following, further sets of findings about the different factors relating to the degree of flexibility and prices of the builders were presented. These findings, when combined, show that multiple skills, simple and general-purpose equipment, low costs and lack of profits enable these builders to provide the aforementioned services.

The findings confirm the correspondence between changes in the output produced by the builders - from low-cost housing to other construction activities - and the changes in the forms of production and labour processes - from petty-commodity to capitalist production, and from handicraft to manufacture and machinofacture - as presented in the model of Table 2.2.

The findings also highlight the limitations of this model. An examination of the repair and maintenance of middle- and high-cost housing shows that low-cost housing is not the only niche in the construction market dominated by petty-commodity production. This is a situation not encompassed by the model. The repair and maintenance of middle- and high-cost housing is an intermediate stage in the movement from low-cost housing production, on the one side, and capitalist production, on the other. Therefore, the conceptual model of the continuum of production presented in Table 2.2 is now modified in Table 3.3 to encapsulate these changes. This model is based on the empirical findings. Once the labour process related to post-fordism (which is depicted in Table 2.2) is not part of such findings, it does not appear in Table 3.3. For the sake of simplification, it also will not appear in the tables referent to similar models which are shown in the following chapters.

Table 3.3
Revised model of Table 2.2: the continuum of production including form of production, labour process and product

labour	PCP	Handicraft
process	CP	Elementary manufacture
	ACP	Advanced manufacture to machinofacture
product	PCP	Low-cost housing and repair of higher cost buildings
	CP and ACP	Construction of complete higher cost buildings

Key:

PCP - petty-commodity production
CP   - capitalist production
ACP - advanced capitalist production

The present chapter concludes the analysis of the capacity of petty-commodity builders to produce low-cost housing. As shown in Chapter 2, such builders face problems which limit their capacity for growth. These problems will be analyzed in the following chapters.

4 Constraints on growth: Equipment and labour capacity

The second basic question posed by this book is the following: *what are the constraints on capitalization faced by petty-commodity builders, and how does their removal affect the participation of the builders in the provision of low-cost housing?* This question will be answered by reference to the obstacles to access to four specific factors: equipment, labour and managerial capacity, and credit. The present chapter deals specifically with the first two. The question above presented is stated here in their specific context: *What are the constraints on capitalization faced by petty-commodity builders in terms of obstacles to access to equipment and to labour capacity, and how does their removal affect the participation of the builders in the provision of low-cost housing?* This chapter will first present a conceptual analysis, followed by empirical data from the activities of the builders introduced in the previous chapter.

Equipment in petty-commodity and capitalist production

The central issues discussed in this section are: the differential between petty-commodity and capitalist builders in terms of equipment, the explanation for this differential, the inaccessibility of petty-commodity builders to equipment necessary to commence capitalist production, the drive of petty-commodity builders to overcome this situation, and its consequences for low-cost housing production.

The difference between the sets of equipment used in petty-commodity and in capitalist production was analyzed in the previous chapter. It was discovered that petty-commodity producers use a set of simple, multi-purpose tools to carry out their artisanal labour process. Capitalist producers, on the other hand, use specialized tools in their process of manufacture, in order to benefit from division of labour and economies of scale. The use of this equipment becomes of greater importance when the labour process changes from manufacture to machinofacture. Tools are then substituted by machines, which are used to increase productivity even further.

Having established a differential between petty-commodity and capitalist producers, the aim now is to understand why the former are restricted from acquiring the equipment necessary to entail capitalist production. The framework adopted by this book reveals a number of possibilities. These include the unavailability of equipment, the financial constraints faced by petty-commodity producers, and lack of access to alternatives such as: second-hand equipment, renovation of scrap, gifts from capitalists who are leaving the country, and hiring.

Obviously, if the tools necessary to establish capitalist production are unobtainable, the growth of petty-commodity producers will be prevented. However, this does not apply to those countries where capitalist production is widespread, for the equipment in question has to be available somehow.

The constraint mostly emphasised in the petty-commodity production literature is lack of financial means to acquire equipment (e.g. Bienefeld, 1979; Gerry, 1979; Le Brun and Gerry, 1975; Scott, 1979). Alternative ways by which petty-commodity producers occasionally overcome this problem include the purchase of second-hand equipment, the recuperation of scrap or spare parts, or the receipt of equipment as gifts from departing expatriates for whom a petty-commodity producer used to work as a labourer (Gerry, 1979; Le Brun and Gerry, 1975). However, if these alternative schemes were extensively available, access to equipment would not be a growth constraint for petty-commodity producers. Thus, it can be stated that petty-commodity producers do not have the financial means to acquire the equipment necessary to establish capitalist production which are available on a wide scale. It is necessary to give emphasis to a 'wide scale', because a limited amount of equipment may be available (e.g. cheap, second-hand one). However, this equipment could only secure the development of a small number of petty-commodity producers.

The last point about the alternative schemes regards equipment for hire. As already noted, it is a widespread practice in the building industry. However, if petty-commodity producers do not have access to equipment, it means that they could not hire them. Hire companies normally require a deposit, which a petty-commodity builder may not be able to pay. However, even if this builder manages to get the money for the deposit, he still needs socio-economic references as proof of his reliability as a client before being able to hire anything. In most cases, petty-commodity builders are unable to obtain such references since they are not registered units of production, have no fixed income, and often do not even have a formal address.

In sum, the basic point extracted from the different possibilities analyzed is that petty-commodity producers do not have the financial means and socio-economic references to acquire the tools necessary to establish capitalist production which are available on a wide scale.

This book assumes, as shown in Chapter 2, that petty-commodity builders have a tendency towards capitalization. If they do not move along the continuum towards a capitalist form of production, it is not due to a lack of motivation, but by reason of the existence of constraints such as lack of equipment. Thus, access to equipment necessary to establish capitalist production opens up growth possibilities for these builders - with the reminder that it is only a partial solution, once other constraints also need to be removed.

However, as noted in the previous chapter, capitalist builders are not capable of producing low-cost housing. Thus, the move of a given builder along the continuum towards capitalist production implies the loss of the characteristics which made him capable of catering for the demands of the low-income people. A conceptual model was put forward in Chapter 2, incorporating the changes in, and correspondence between, different forms of production, labour processes, and products which are necessary to the process of transformation of units of production. This model is now resumed in Table 4.1, with the inclusion of the changes which concern equipment.

Table 4.1
Conceptual model of the continuum of production including form of production, labour process, product and equipment

labour	PCP	Handicraft
process	CP	Elementary manufacture
	ACP	Advanced manufacture to machinofacture
product	PCP	Low-cost housing
	CP and ACP	Other types of buildings
equipment	PCP	Simple, general purpose
	CP and ACP	Specialized equipment

Key:

PCP - petty-commodity production
CP   - capitalist production
ACP - advanced capitalist production

Labour capacity in petty-commodity and capitalist production

The move along the continuum from petty-commodity to capitalist production in terms of the labour force is seen as a gradual evolution from casual apprenticeship towards stable wage employment. This notion is supported by Gerry and Scott, and indicates that there is a differentiation in conditions of employment (Gerry, 1979; Scott, 1979). This variation has actually been used to support the definition of petty-commodity and capitalist producers. However, the differentiation in the labour force goes beyond conditions of employment. In that, it is necessary to distinguish between the transformation of a petty-commodity *master* producer into a wage labourer, and the transformation of a petty-commodity *labourer* into a wage labourer.

The literature on the development of the labour process supports the idea of the de-skilling of labour which occurs during the transition from handicraft to manufacture, and from manufacture to machinofacture (e.g. Brighton Labour Process Group, 1977;

Liberaki, 1988; Marx, 1977). However, in the transfer from handicraft to manufacture, de-skilling does not take place within the labour force. The above-mentioned authors refer to the master artisan, who is engaged in all stages of production, and loses some of her/his skills when s/he ceases to be the head of a handicraft unit of production and joins a manufacturing unit as a labourer, in which capacity s/he will produce only part of a product. However, the artisan is not considered here as a labourer in handicraft, but as the master of the unit of production. Although directly engaged in the process of production, s/he owns the means of production, heads the unit and often has labourers working under her/his control. Therefore, it is not the handicraft labourer who is de-skilled. In fact, the labour force engaged in handicraft needs to acquire new skills in order to work in manufacture.

As already shown, the workforce engaged in handicraft is made up of journeymen and apprentices. Although journeymen may on occasion have an independent function, in general they support the work of the master him/herself, as do the apprentices. In manufacture, the work carried out by the handicraft master him/herself is transferred to wage-labourers. Therefore, wage-labourers perform tasks not undertaken by apprentices and journeymen - and thus have more skills than the latter. Thus, actually a process of skilling of the labour force occurs in the transition from handicraft to manufacture. As shown in Chapter 2, the elementary stage of manufacture embodies the onset of capitalist production. Therefore, skilled labourers are a constraint for the move from petty-commodity to capitalist production, if the petty-commodity producers lack the financial means necessary to hire such labourers.

The conceptual model of the theoretical framework from Tables 2.1 and 2.2 is now resumed again in Table 4.2, with the insertion of labour capacity. Assuming that a petty-commodity builder has a drive to move in the continuum towards capitalist production, access to skilled labour will give him the opportunity to develop and capitalize. Nevertheless, as already noted, the move in the continuum implies that the builders will not be capable of producing low-cost housing any more.

In summary, the argument about labour skills as well as equipment developed so far shows that: (i) petty-commodity builders use simple, general purpose tools and unskilled labour in the production of low-cost housing, (ii) capitalist production requires the use of specialized tools and/or machines as well as a skilled labour force to accomplish the specific tasks to be carried out in each stage of the construction process, (iii) petty-commodity producers have neither the financial means nor the socio-economic references necessary to acquire the equipment and to hire the labour force which is required in capitalist production, and (iv) access to such equipment and labour force and the consequent movement of the builders towards capitalist production imply their loss of the ability to produce low-cost housing in developing countries.

The builders

The above reasoning is substantiated by empirical findings from the activities of the builders introduced in the previous chapter. Equipment and labour will be examined sequentially.

Table 4.2
Conceptual model of the continuum of production including form of production, labour process, product and labour capacity

labour process	PCP	Handicraft
	CP	Elementary manufacture
	ACP	Advanced manufacture to machinofacture
product	PCP	Low-cost housing
	CP and ACP	Other types of buildings
labour capacity	PCP	Unskilled labour
	CP	Increasing predominance of skilled labour
	ACP	Decrease in skills

Key:

PCP - petty-commodity production
CP - capitalist production
ACP - advanced capitalist production

Equipment

Equipment for low-cost housing production Data about this issue was presented in the previous chapter. However, in order to avoid the need for cross-checking, the main findings will be recapitulated. Some forty different types of tools are used in the construction of low-cost housing. Only a few are used in just one specific stage of construction, namely: auger, metal level, manual drill, mesh, brushes, painting tray, spatula, reinforcement bar and steel shear. All the others are used in different stages (sometimes even outside construction). They constitute simple, multi-purpose tools.

Equipment for other activities An analysis of builders working outside low-income settlements revealed three main types of activities: repair and maintenance of middle- and high-cost housing, construction of complete single housing units and/or other types of buildings, and construction of several housing units and/or other types of buildings in parallel. A comparative analysis of these activities revealed that there is an increasing specialization in the equipment used.

The equipment used in low-cost housing construction is also used in repair and maintenance of middle- and high-cost housing. However, this work also requires other equipment. They are all specialized, and include marble cutter, grooving plane, monkey wrench, threading dye, power drill, circular table power saw, sanding machine, power planer, manual double saw, grooving plane, chisel. Like low-cost housing construction, the repair and maintenance of middle- and high-cost housing is carried out through petty-commodity production. Yet, it entails an increase in the number of specialized equipment.

The construction of complete single housing units or other buildings requires the specialized tools above mentioned as well as others. This new equipment can be divided in two groups. The first is specialized equipment which, like the set used in repair and maintenance of middle- and high-cost housing, is used for activities not required in low-cost housing production - e.g. bench vise, power sander, concrete pistol, van. Thus, they *add* to the existing set. The second group consists of specialized tools which *substitute* for a number of the simple and multi-purpose equipment used in low-cost housing production. They include, for instance, steel cutter machine, pincers, circular table power saw, handbarrow, concrete mixer, pneumatic drill.

Several of the multi-purpose tools used in low-cost housing construction are still used in the production of complete units (e.g. builder square, trowel, wheelbarrow, flooring board). However, several other are supplanted by specialized ones.

The concurrent construction of several housing units and/or other buildings requires the use of further specialized equipment, in order to meet an additional increase in the scale of production (for instance, pile hammer, scaffolding, winch, vibrating tamper).

In sum, the passage from the petty-commodity production of low-cost housing to the capitalist production of other types of buildings entails an increase in the degree of specialization of the equipment used, both in relative and absolute terms - substitution of multi-purpose equipment for specialized ones, and acquisition of additional specialized equipment.

The process of acquisition of equipment The aim here is to verify that petty-commodity producers do not have the financial means and socio-economic references to acquire the equipment necessary to establish capitalist production which are available on a wide scale. By way of comparison, the acquisition of the equipment used in the production of low-cost housing will be examined first.

Two means of acquiring the equipment used in low-cost housing production have been identified: purchase through savings, and a combination of inheritance and savings. None of the builders experienced difficulties in acquiring the equipment in question. The case of the exclusive builder Alberto illustrates this statement.

Alberto kept no record of the precise date on which he bought each tool, or of the price he paid for it. However, a comparison between the present price of the equipment that he bought after his initial training - Cr$9,020.00 altogether - and his average revenue in low-cost housing production - approximately Cr$8,750.00 per month (Cr$350.00 per day) - shows that the former is only fractionally more than the latter (1.03 times). According to Alberto, these were bought little by little over a period of three years. According to these figures, Alberto would have spent Cr$250.56 per month on average on equipment, which is only 2.86% of his monthly revenue. The relationship between the price of the equipment acquired by each builder producing low-cost housing at the time of the field work and his monthly revenue in low-income settlements varies from 0.4 to 2.16.

However, the acquisition of the equipment for the purpose of other construction activities is a different matter. The exclusive builder Amin, for instance, gave the following testimony:

The pay that I get from the work here [in low-income settlements] is not great, you know... I can hardly keep on going... New tools would help... But how can I buy more tools, then?... A power drill for instance would be very handy, save me a lot of work... But it costs more than what I earn in a whole month, there is no way.

The other exclusive builders had similar obstacles to the purchase of equipment. They were also constrained to hire equipment, as exemplified by the following account given by Evandro:

I went to three hire shops, and it was always the same story... Then comes the avalanche of documents required, all types of identification cards, proof of address, proof of non-criminal record, bank account, proof of source of income, references from people who would back me in case of default, fill in forms, pay a deposit and present other documents.

The exclusive builders revealed the existence of alternative ways of acquiring equipment, including the use of cheaper, second-hand ones, informal hiring, and borrowing. However, these options were available only on a restricted and random basis, which was insufficient for the support of construction work outside low-income settlements. The difficulties involved in acquiring equipment for this work are further illustrated by the case of those builders who work outside low-income settlements. For example, the total cost of the set of equipment used by the transitional builder Elisio to build for upper-classes was Cr$54,000.00. This is equivalent to 4.32 times the monthly revenue of a builder earning Cr$500.00 a day in low-cost housing production. According to Elisio, he could not have afforded equipment worth Cr$54,000.00 when he was working in low-income settlements full-time. The process of acquisition of this equipment is illustrated in the following quotation by the mixed builder Tomas:

I could not purchase this equipment during the period in which I was working full-time in low-cost housing production... But I eventually managed to take a step outside the low-income settlements, to carry out some small services in Lourdes and Santo Agostinho [upper-middle class neighbourhoods in Belo Horizonte], which I could carry out with the tools that I already had... As I have told you before, this work is better paid than the construction of low-cost housing, and the extra money which I received from it has allowed me to buy the new tools which I told you about, in order to expand my new activities in Lourdes and Santo Agostinho.

The hybrid, semi-capitalist, capitalist and advanced capitalist builders also need further equipment to carry out the construction of complete residences for middle- and high-income households. The hybrid builder Baltazar, for example, had all the equipment used by Elisio, plus a steel cutting machine, pincers, a circular power saw, a bench vice, a handbarrow, a concrete mixer, a pneumatic drill (see Chapter 3). The present cost of this set of equipment is the equivalent to approximately twenty times what Baltazar would gain in a month of full-time work in low-cost housing production. In his words:

> Twenty times my revenue in low-cost housing production. How could I have bought them at that time?... I could only do it after I had began to move outside low-income settlements, using the basic set of tools which I already had... Another factor which helped me a lot was the availability of construction equipment for hire... This allowed me to use it, until I had enough capital to buy my own.

The issue of hiring was developed further by Baltazar:

> When working full-time in low-cost housing production, I had a lot of problems to rent tools... I did not even have a decent outfit to go to the shop, and you know how these things are, first impression... Besides, I did not have much contacts... Now I can give the name of a number of rich clients as references, and it makes a difference... My bank account now is better than before... The shop does not ask me to sign so many papers any more, they trust me now.

The other hybrid builders as well as the semi-capitalist, capitalist and advanced capitalist builders had a similar experience when purchasing and hiring equipment. Thus, the main finding is that none of the builders were able to acquire the equipment necessary for capitalist production while working only in low-cost housing construction. They only managed to buy these tools after they started working outside low-income settlements. However, as will be shown now, the access to equipment necessary to establish capitalist production and the consequent movement of the builders along the continuum of production imply in their loss of the ability to produce low-cost housing.

The effects of improving the supply of equipment As indicated before, the mere provision of equipment used in capitalist production is not sufficient to enable builders to move away from petty-commodity production. Thus, in the following text, it must always be remembered that the provision of equipment is only one relevant factor and plays only a partial role in influencing the development of builders.

This book uses two ways of assessing the development of each builder: *policy-like situations*, and *scenarios*. The first way consists of the assessment of those builders who managed to acquire equipment required to work outside low-income settlements. The data obtained from this method of assessment are used to sustain the proposition that, if policies which replicate these circumstances are implemented, other builders will follow a similar path. The second way consists of tracing speculative future actions which would be taken by each builder, if the equipment in question could be provided.

Part of the data necessary to substantiate the policy-like situations has already been presented in Chapter 3 - e.g. the inability of builders to produce low-cost housing after having acquired equipment necessary to carry out other activities. At any rate, the major findings from this material will be recapitulated.

Mixed and transitional builders acquired the equipment necessary to carry out repair and maintenance in middle- and high-income residences via a process of saving through simple operations, already described. As noted in Chapter 3, the process of acquisition of this equipment resulted in a partial or entire move away from low-income settlements. For example, the transitional builder Elisio declared:

> Now I have the tools to work for the rich, and, frankly, I am not interested in working for the poor any more... Now I can charge Cr$1,100.00 per day for my services. No one in a low-income neighbourhood can pay that.

This quotation illustrates that Elisio lost one of the basic characteristics which, in the past, enabled him to produce low-cost housing: a price for his services which satisfied the limited budgets of the low-income people.

Mixed builders still work part-time in low-income settlements, but, as shown in Chapter 3, they are inclined to expand their activities into middle- and high-income neighbourhoods, as opposed to concentrating on low-cost housing production. Hybrid, semi-capitalist, capitalist and advanced capitalist builders have moved away from petty-commodity towards capitalist production (either partially or totally). This move was initially prevented by their lack of access to appropriate equipment. However, with savings gathered from the repair and maintenance of middle- and high-cost housing, they were eventually able to buy some of this equipment. They also acquired the credentials necessary to hire others. Thus, they completed the set necessary to establish capitalist production. However, as noted in Chapter 3, the acquisition of this equipment led to the loss of those factors which had previously enabled them to produce low-cost housing. Testimonies of these builders revealed the way in which they shifted away from low-cost housing production. Much of the equipment in question can only be used in larger-scale construction, and to substitute tools used in low-cost housing production. To give one example, a concrete mixer is only used for a minimum of 1 cubic meter of concrete. However, the construction of a low-cost residence requires smaller quantities (in each stage). The acquisition of the equipment used in capitalist production requires an investment which has to be recovered. This consequently increases the costs of the builder's services. On a larger commission, this cost is counteracted by economies of scale, which push the unit price of the product down. However, economies of scale are impossible in the small-scale and often interrupted activities in low-income settlements, whereas the costs of the equipment must nevertheless be embodied into the prices of services (Chapters 2 and 3).

In sum, the use of the specialized equipment required to set up capitalist production entails the loss of the degree of flexibility necessary to deliver small volumes of discontinuous output with a price which meets the atomized disbursements of the low-income people. Builders who repair and maintain middle- and high-cost housing still have flexibility which allows them to shift back quickly to low-cost housing production, when necessary. However, when a manufacturing process is set up to produce complete residences, this flexibility is lost. Testimonies from the capitalist and advanced capitalist builders, presented in Chapter 3, confirmed this situation. As they have a continuous demand for the construction of complete buildings, they lose the capacity to produce low-cost housing entirely.

Thus, an examination of the case of the builders who ceased to produce low-cost housing either partially or fully, gives an indication of the possible effect of a policy which substitutes the process of acquisition of the equipment in question. The scenarios regarding the plans of the builders who produce low-cost housing will be examined next.

The acquisition of new equipment appealed to a number of the builders interviewed. The exclusive builder Juvenal was planning to work as a specialist in finishing. Evandro and Ronan aimed to work in the repair and maintenance of middle- and high-cost housing, and eventually expand their services. The hybrid builder Rafael was planning to become a speculative builder and landlord. Augusto planned to set up a unit specializing in electrical and water services and eventually expand his scope of services even further. Baltazar was willing to increase his participation in the production of complete residences. All these builders needed additional equipment to realize their plans and/or wanted to purchase the equipment that they had to hire.

A number of possible procedures for the provision of the equipment were discussed with them. These include financing, provision of second-hand equipment, recuperation of scrap, the setting up of a cooperative of builders to acquire equipment more cheaply, and hire. The position of the builders regarding such possibilities is illustrated by the following quote from Rafael:

> Most schemes have problems... It could be too dangerous to acquire new equipment without having the means to repay. You know how unreliable construction is... The ideal situation would be a scheme which would allow me to make some kind of flexible repayments, which would vary according to revenues... If my income rises, I pay more, and I prefer this situation in order to get rid of the loan as soon as possible... But if my income falls, I should be allowed to pay less... I am not so sure about other solutions... The purchase of second-hand equipment sure helps, but I have already used it... In order to improve it, it would be necessary to cheapen its cost, and then we go back to the matter of money... This question of fixing scrap equipment is not a good idea... It is very difficult to make good use of scrap, because builders use it until they are completely ruined, and one would also need expertise to fix them, which I do not have... The idea of a cooperative of builders to buy or hire equipment cheaply, or perhaps even to lend, would be advantageous, but very difficult to implement... We work in a very random way, you know. I have never seen builders like me organized together, and I do not believe that it could be done... Each one is worried only about his own business... One thing that really helps us is the availability of equipment for hire. It is very handy to know that the equipment is there whenever we need it... Perhaps if more equipment for hire was available, and access to it was easier, and cheaper prices, it would be a great help to us.

In sum, the aforementioned builders were willing to accept a policy of provision of equipment, as long as it conforms to some conditions. These builders would use this

69

policy as a support to establish themselves in activities such as the repair and maintenance of middle- and high-cost housing, specialized subcontracted work, and/or construction of complete residences. Some of these activities would still be carried out using a petty-commodity form of production. However, in all cases, a departure from low-cost housing production would occur.

The case of the remaining builders who work in low-cost housing production is different. The exclusive builders Alberto, Amin and João Pedro, the mixed builders Tomas and Dorcelino and the hybrid builder Waldemar regarded the expansion of their businesses as too risky, and therefore were not willing to invest in new equipment. However, they were not willing to carry on producing low-cost housing for a long time either, due to the uncertainties of this activity.

Summarizing the findings regarding equipment: the policy-like situations of builders already engaged in capitalist production and the scenarios of builders who are willing to accept the provision of new equipment confirm the reasoning about the movement of the builders towards capitalist production and their departure from low-income settlements. However, the scenarios also revealed a number of builders who were not willing to acquire new equipment. Their cases do not confirm the above reasoning. However, it must be remembered that these builders are not prepared to increase their participation in the production of low-cost housing in any event. Thus, while the provision of equipment does not affect some builders, it leads others to work away from low-income settlements, so that the overall result is a reduction of the participation of builders in the production of low-cost housing.

The following sections relate to the other element (labour capacity) analyzed in this chapter. The sequence of the analysis is similar to that of equipment.

Labour capacity

Labour for low-cost housing production This section aims to demonstrate that petty-commodity builders use unskilled labour to produce low-cost housing and that labourers merely support the work carried out by builders. In this context, attention is drawn to the skills of the labour force hired by builders, and not to the skills of the builders themselves. There are two basic types of labourer working with builders in the production of low-cost housing: apprentices and journeymen. An illustration of the role of the first of these is given by the exclusive builder Juvenal:

> My construction work here is actually carried out by me. The apprentices just help me to do some basic things... The apprentices are generally teenagers, or, sometimes, twenty-something years-old at the most... They are people who hang around the low-income settlements, and do not have any qualification or job... I hire them to perform the crudest activities in my construction contracts... They only work with their arms, not with their brains. They only carry out the work which does not need skills.

Regarding the journeymen, the hybrid builder Augusto stated the following:

In the process of labour training in the [formal] construction industry, one enters as a trainee in a given craft, like bricklaying, electrical installations, water installations, etc... After a certain period of training, he is upgraded to the post of semi-official... After a further period, he is finally upgraded to the post of full-official... My journeymen are generally semi-officials who help me after hours in order to earn some more money, or who lost their jobs, and then work with builders like me until they find another firm where they can complete their training... They have more skills than the apprentices... I do not use journeymen much... I hire them when the client can afford to pay a larger labour force, and then the work is accomplished more quickly... The size of the workforce and the pace of the work in low-cost housing construction depends very much on the pocket of the client, you know... I never use full-officials as journeymen, because such people demand higher pay to perform their activities, or prefer to get their own contracts directly with clients rather than to work for builders like myself.

As shown, apprentices are unskilled labourers. However, the journeymen, which are hired eventually, are semi-skilled labourers. Thus, the above findings show that petty-commodity builders use a majority (not a totality) of unskilled labourers to produce low-cost housing.

Labour for other activities This section shows that capitalist manufacture production requires a labour capacity to accomplish the specific tasks to be carried out at each stage of the construction process. It presents data about the builders who work outside low-income settlements.

The mixed and transitional builders still use a petty-commodity form of production on a full-time basis and their labour force is similar to that used in low-cost housing production. However, the case of the hybrid, semi-capitalist, capitalist and advanced capitalist builders is different. They need labourers with broader skills for the construction of complete buildings using a capitalist process. The semi-capitalist builder Joaquim gave an account of the differences between the two types of work in which he is involved; namely, the repair and maintenance of middle- and high-cost housing, and the construction of complete buildings:

When I just carry out refurbishment work, it is me and one or two assistants... They deal only with the very basic things, I deal with the bulky work, just like the way I used to work in squats and other poor areas... The construction of an entire residence is a different story... There, I just supervise. I hire professionals who are in control of the different parts of the work... I need almost a dozen types of specialized workers, you see... Let's see, if we divide the construction into foundations and structure; walls and panelling; roofing; plastering; doors and windows; flooring; installations; paintings and finishing: I need bricklayers and reinforcement fixers for the foundations and structure; bricklayers and painters for walls and panelling; carpenters for roofing; bricklayers, plasterers and tile setters for plastering; carpenters, jointer, bricklayers for doors and windows; for flooring a

71

carpenter, bricklayer and floor fixer; plumber and electricians for installations; painters and bricklayers for painting and finishing.

Like Joaquim, the hybrid and semi-capitalist builders also carry out the construction of single buildings, using a capitalist manufacture process. Their cases replicate that of Joaquim in terms of their labour requirements. The advanced capitalist builders, in turn, need even more workers to carry out the construction of a series of horizontal housing units and/or apartment blocks concomitantly, through a process of manufacture *cum* machinofacture. They require all the labour specialities mentioned above, but also need others to carry out tasks such as large-scale earthwork, the operation and maintenance of machines, special installations.

The size of the permanent workforce of the builders varies according to the demand for volume of work. Some of them subcontract a number of workers. Nevertheless, whether a given task is performed by a fixed or subcontracted worker, builders who use a capitalist manufacture form of production need the labour capacity to carry out specific jobs at each stage of the construction process.

The process of acquisition of labour This section analyzes the process of acquisition of labour required for petty-commodity and for capitalist production.

In terms of the financial aspect of hiring the labourers, two situations were found to exist in relation to the production of low-cost housing: builders who do not spend any money on their workforce, and those who have saved enough to support their labourers for a period of between one and two weeks.

The first situation refers to exclusive builders. Alberto stated the following:

> Unfortunately, I have not been able to save much money from my work, and I cannot pay my workers out of my own pocket... My first priority was to buy tools. Without them I cannot work, but without labourers I can still work... I only carry out those activities which the client can afford... If the individual hires me and delays my payment, I can cope alone for one week or two with the help of relatives and friends; but he has to give me at least enough to pay the apprentices or a journeyman, in case the job requires them... If I had some money to pay the workers, I would probably get more work here, I would not be afraid of risk... But there are a lot of minor jobs now, that I can do alone, and there are clients who can at least advance enough money for me to pay my assistants.

The second situation refers to the case of the remaining builders who work in low-income settlements. As the mixed builder Tomas exemplifies:

> In the construction industry workers are paid weekly, every Friday, and I too adopt this procedure... My clients advance money to pay my services and that of the workforce every week, but there have been cases of a delay in payment, because, you know, these people are very poor... Sometimes something unexpected turns up, they run out of money... If the contract is very small, one or two days, then it is O.K., but there are larger contracts, and then the

72

troubles appear... When this happens, if it is something serious, I interrupt the construction work, dismiss the workers, and go to another client, until the former client is able to start construction again... But sometimes it is just a delay of one week or so, and in this case I prefer to pay my workers during this period out of my own pocket and be reimbursed later, to avoid all the trouble of having to dismantle my site apparatus, and later having to set it up again... But to do this, I need to have some money in reserve... I have never worked with more than two apprentices and one journeyman at the same time; usually I work with less than that... The weekly payment of this workforce is no more than Cr$4,200.00... I need less than Cr$9,000.00 for two weeks for this work team.

Tomas compares the reserve fund for the workforce with the acquisition of equipment:

I was saving for the workforce like I was saving for my tools, little by little... I did not buy the tools at the same time, and without them my range of work was limited. I did not need to hire many people, really... And when I started to buy my tools, here and there, I took care to keep a little bit of the money for my workers... And I need less money for the workers.

The reserve fund for the workforce was smaller than the savings necessary to buy the equipment. The set of equipment used by Tomas in low-cost housing production was worth approximately Cr$35,000.00 converted into prices current at the time of the field work (including those acquired during his training). As already mentioned, he needed less than Cr$9,000.00 by way of a reserve fund to pay the workforce.

The other mixed and the hybrid builders gave a similar account of their experiences, although with variations in their weekly payment of the workforce, and in the amount of time that they were prepared to wait for a client who was in arrears to resume payments. The weekly payment for the maximum workforce used by each builder in low-cost housing production varied from Cr$2,640.00 to Cr$3,900.00, and the time which they were prepared to wait varied from one to two weeks. The resulting figures show that Augusto, Waldemar and Dorcelino were prepared to spend around Cr$3,500.00 on their workforce in low-cost housing production, Rafael Cr$4,000.00, and Baltazar Cr$6,000.00. All of them saved their respective reserve funds through a process similar to that of Tomas. At the same time, they spent approximately the same amount as Tomas for the purchase of the equipment. The transitional, semi-capitalist, capitalist and advanced capitalist builders gave also a similar account, regarding their needs in terms of a reserve fund to pay their workforce involved in their past low-cost housing production.

The process and problems involved in the acquisition of the labour capacity necessary for capitalist production will now be examined. As has already been shown, the repair and maintenance of middle- and high-cost housing requires the same labour capacity as that used in low-cost housing production. Therefore, a builder who produces low-cost housing is not prevented, in terms of his labour capacity, from carrying out this work as well. Even exclusive builders, who keep no reserve fund, would be able to carry out those tasks which do require assistants, or those for which the client is able to pay the workers in advance. However, as also noted, lack of access to the labour capacity required for the capitalist production of complete dwellings constrained the exclusive builders. The hybrid and semi-capitalist builders, in turn, have had access to this labour capacity. However, they have complained about fluctuations in the availability of specialized labour. In the words of the hybrid builder Augusto:

> The possibility of finding good labourers varies... If the construction business is bad, then there is more unemployment, and there are plenty of good men available... However, when construction is booming, they all go, and it is exactly when construction is booming that I have more opportunity to get a larger contract, which needs more workers!

This situation derives from the fact that hybrid and semi-capitalist builders do not in general have sufficient demand to start the construction of a finished building immediately after the completion of the previous one. They dismiss their workforce, and resume work in low-income settlements or undertake the repair and maintenance of middle- and high-cost housing. When they win another contract for a complete house, they have to hire labourers again. The capitalist and advanced capitalist builders are in a better position since they have a permanent core of workers. However, in terms of labour capacity, availability of workers is not the main problem faced by any builder who is willing to establish capitalist production. As Baltazar said:

> I have told you that I am prepared to spend up to Cr$6,000.00 to cover delays in the payment of my workforce involved in low-cost housing construction... In the construction of full houses for middle-income families, I have more workers than in low-income settlements... I have from four to eight people on a site... I do not need more money than to cover eight people, being three officials and five trainees, for two weeks.

The sum of money mentioned by Baltazar is the equivalent of Cr$30,091.60, at prices current at the time of the field work. When confronted with this figure, he went on to say:

> If I save little by little, one day of course I could make Cr$30,091.60 even while working in low-income settlements alone. But there are two problems. One is that it would take a long, long time... It took me more than five years to buy my tools so that I could build low-cost housing, if I include my time of training... This amount now, about Cr$30.000,00, is more than that... The other problem, which is much worse, is that money in the bank is always a problem for a poor builder. When I buy my tools, it is O.K., but if I save money, there are all sorts of pressures, like from my wife, and even I may feel tempted to spend it... If it is just money to pay a few apprentices, it is one thing. But about Cr$30,000.00 in the bank, is different... My life has not been easy, you know. My family and I have had many problems... I opened a

savings account many times, but had to withdraw the money a little later and close the account... It was difficult to save, we always had to tighten our belts.

In the words of Baltazar, his movement into the middle- and high-income market was fundamental in giving him access to the labour force necessary to establish capitalist production for two reasons: savings and credit.

> Only when I started catering for richer families, that I could ease the belt a little bit, so to speak. I could save enough to be able to hire skilled people... I would say that the acquisition of my personnel is more or less similar to that of equipment. Part of the problem was solved through my own savings, but the other part was solved differently. With equipment, the solution was to hire them, when I needed something specific that I did not already own. But I cannot rent labourers in the same way... So, in an emergency, I had to borrow some money... I could not borrow when working in low-income settlements, for nobody would lend to me. The people I know in these areas do not even have enough for themselves, let alone to lend... There are indeed some who manage to lend, but as a poor builder, I did not have the credentials to borrow. These guys want some guarantee that I can pay them back, and I could not do it... After mingling with rich people, many things happened. My own standard of living increased, and I acquired a stable clientele. This is very important when you want to borrow money. You have to convince people that you can pay back... Sometimes I also borrowed from my own clients. They got to know me well, to trust me, and Cr$10,000.00, Cr$20,000.00, Cr$30,000.00 means nothing to them, they could easily lend to me.

The funds that the other hybrid builders and the semi-capitalist builder needed to procure the workforce necessary for capitalist production were in the same range of that of Baltazar, varying from Cr$26,504.80 to Cr$37,051.40. All these builders declared that they had been able to save money for this purpose after they started working in the repair and maintenance of middle- and high-cost housing. Like Baltazar, the hybrid builders Augusto and Waldemar and the semi-capitalist Joaquim also relied on occasional borrowing to complement their funds.

The capitalist builders, Wander and José, were found to need a larger fund than that of the aforementioned builders - i.e. Cr$60,000.00 and Cr$80,000.00 respectively. They require larger funds because they carry out several contracts concomitantly. Their difficulties in amassing such funds while working full-time in low-income settlements were greater than those of the semi-capitalist and hybrid builders. The capitalist builders have a further problem, as illustrated by Wander:

> I lose money when I lose workers... If they do not feel that they will be paid on time, they might leave me, and then I have to go through all the procedure of recruiting other men and training them... My workers are already used to my way of doing things, so I do not want to lose them.

Both José and Wander relied on borrowing and savings accumulated from their work in the middle- and high-income markets. The advanced capitalist builders, in turn, needed a much larger fund in order to carry out their speculative building work. They have to pay the workforce involved in the construction of a given residential unit before the client purchases it. In the case of the housing units built by Gastão, presented in Chapter 3, his expenditure on the workforce, at prices adjusted to the time of the field work, was Cr$459,616.20, Cr$424,806.0, Cr$533,568.00 and Cr$477,112.00 respectively for the following units: two bedroom residences (60 square meters); two bedroom flats (60 square meters); three bedroom residences (80 square meters) and three bedroom flats (80 square meters). The magnitude of Gustavo's developments and the funds required for his workforce are similar to those of Gastão. Gustavo acquired his funds through three different ways: a system of condominium, investment by acquaintances, and his own savings and accumulation. Gastão acquired his funds through the second and third of these ways. However, these builders managed to acquire them only after abandoning the production of low-cost housing.

In short, none of the builders have been able to acquire the labour capacity necessary to establish capitalist production while working full-time in low-income settlements. Although the shortage of skilled labourers during times of boom was mentioned, the main problem was that the builders were unable to amass a reserve fund necessary to pay the workers. They only found ways to pay such labourers after they started working outside low-income settlements. Now, the way access to labour capacity required for capitalist production affected the construction of low-cost housing will be examined.

The effects of improving the supply of labour The effect of provision of labour capacity will be analyzed in a similar fashion to the earlier analysis of the provision of equipment, through policy-like situations and scenarios.

As already noted, mixed and transitional builders are able to carry out the repair and maintenance of middle- and high-cost housing with the same labour capacity as that required for low-cost housing production. However, their involvement in this type of work entails an increase in their fees, thus jeopardizing their activities in low-income settlements. Semi-capitalist and hybrid builders partially moved from petty-commodity to capitalist production, whereas capitalist and advanced capitalist builders moved entirely. This movement was initially constrained by lack of access to appropriate labour capacity. However, savings gathered from the repair and maintenance of middle- and high-cost housing eventually allowed the formation of a reserve fund with which to pay the workforce. Advanced capitalist builders also rely on payments from a scheme of condominium, and from borrowing from acquaintances.

Statements from hybrid, semi-capitalist, capitalist and advanced capitalist builders revealed the way in which they were driven away from low-cost housing production. They needed specialized and a dearer workforce in order to set up manufacture production. Similarly to the case of specialized equipment, the insertion of this workforce is appropriate for a large-scale operation, in which the division of labour and increase in productivity counteract the rigidity and structure of costs. However, as already noted, it is not operative for the production of low-cost housing. The builders lose the flexibility to deliver small volumes of a discontinuous output with a price which meets the erratic disbursements of the low-income people. A statement given by Wander, and presented in Chapter 3 illustrates the situation:

> Although each labourer has a different skill, the firm as a whole functions only in a specific fashion... I pay my workers to carry out specific and connected functions, that is the way we can benefit... I gain from planning at least a medium-scale contract, and then executing it according to the plans... After planning, the execution becomes rigid... I cannot afford to shift constantly from producing one thing to another. This is just when me or my labourers could use diverse skills... But nowadays I gain exactly from not using diverse skills, I gain from using specialized skills.

The cases of the semi-capitalist and hybrid builders revealed that, during the construction of a complete residence, they lose the characteristics which enable them to produce low-cost housing. Although they do not have a continuous demand for complete houses, they already have the labour capacity which enables them to carry out this activity. As a result, they feel inclined to abandon their work in low-income settlements at the first opportunity. The semi-capitalist builder Joaquim, in turn, managed to capture enough demand for repair and maintenance in the middle- and high-income market so that he no longer had to produce low-cost housing. The capitalist and advanced capitalist builders, who have a continuous demand for the construction of complete residences, were found to have lost the capacity to produce low-cost housing entirely.

In short, the cases of these builders who discontinued their production of low-cost housing either partially or entirely reveal the possible effect of a policy which would replace the current process of acquisition of the labour capacity in question.

The scenarios constructed on the basis of the plans of those builders who produce low-cost housing will be examined now. Similarly to the scenarios regarding equipment, the possibility of provision of labour capacity appealed only to some builders. The exclusive builders Juvenal, Evandro and Ronan, and the hybrid builder Rafael welcomed this possibility. However, the exclusive builders Alberto, Amin and João Pedro, the mixed builders Tomas and Dorcelino, and the hybrid builders Waldemar, Augusto and Baltazar did not.

Three major possibilities regarding access to labour capacity were discussed with them: loans to set up a reserve fund, training to increase the pool of skilled workers, and mechanization to decrease the need for skilled workers.

As already shown, Juvenal, Evandro and Ronan were willing to establish themselves in activities such as the repair and maintenance of middle- and high-cost housing, specialist subcontracted work, and/or the construction of complete dwellings. They all recognized the need to form a reserve fund for the payment of the workforce in order to set up capitalist production, although, at the time, they had no clear idea as to the size of the workforce required. They welcomed the possibility of loans, but were sceptical as to the schemes of repayment of them, in similar fashion to their reaction to the scenarios regarding equipment. All these builders hinted to the advantages of flexible repayments, which have already been noted.

The possibility of implementing new training schemes so as to increase the pool of skilled labourers was also welcomed by them, although it seemed less important than the provision of loans. As Juvenal stated:

> Well, if there are more skilled workers available, it sure helps... It would mean less hassle at the time of hiring... But I do not see if this would really influence their wages... There are the trade unions, the government, you know... What I really would like is to spend less on the workers.

The subordinate importance of the training schemes was also shown by the lack of willingness of the builders to help. Juvenal went on to add:

> I cannot allow my workers to go to any sort of training course during the period which I am paying them... I cannot afford that. I think that training is a responsibility of the worker and of the government, not mine.

The third type of scenario did not appeal to these builders. They could not see how they could start off by using more machines than workers. As Ronan showed:

> I do not know what I will be doing in five or ten years. I might be building big things, who knows... But there is no point in mechanizing my production now, there is no demand for that... I see today that even big companies still have a lot of workers. I do not really understand how machines would help me... Even getting support, I want to progress slowly, to be sure of each of my steps... I do not like to go on jumps... And I would still have to pay for the machines, wouldn't I?

At any rate, the scenarios regarding the builders willing to accept a policy of provision of labour capacity reveal that the outcome is a departure from low-cost housing production. The cases of the builders who are not willing to have access to skilled labour force will now be examined.

The exclusive builders Alberto and Amin and the hybrid builder Waldemar, who were willing to engage in wage-work, did not change their plans when the possibility of support for the hire of skilled labour was presented to them. Their attitude regarding access to labour was the same as that regarding access to equipment, already presented. They were neither willing to set up capitalist production, nor to remain working in low-income settlements. The possibility of providing an adequate labour force to enable them to set up a few small-scale teams to increase their production of low-cost housing - as well as their income - changed neither their plans nor those of the other builders. The hybrid builder Tomas, the mixed Dorcelino and the exclusive João Pedro, who do not want to change their activities, were not attracted to the possibility of obtaining skilled labour (nor equipment).

However, the case of the hybrid builders Baltazar and Augusto were different. While they were unwilling to accept the provision of labour, they were interested in provision of equipment. Baltazar did not want to change his present activities, and already had the required workforce - he merely wanted to buy the equipment that he was renting at the time. Augusto, who wanted to set up a small-scale unit of production specialized in installations, did not have a problem of access either to equipment or to labour in a first instance. Later on, he would acquire more equipment, but had no plans to increase his workforce. According to him, any possible change in his workforce could only happen in the long run. Thus, the immediate implementation of this type of policy did not appeal to him.

In short, an examination of the policy-like situations of those builders who carry out capitalist production, and the scenarios of the builders who accepted the provision of labour capacity, confirm the argument about the movement of the builders towards capitalist production and their departure from low-income settlements. The scenarios also unveiled a number of builders who, due to personal circumstances, did not accept policies to support the hire of new labourers. Their cases do not confirm the above argument. However, as the access to skilled labour does not affect some builders, but lead others away from low-income settlements, the overall result was a reduction of the participation of builders in the production of low-cost housing.

Conclusion

In the introduction to the present chapter, one of the two main questions of this book was restated in the form of a particular question, specifically related to equipment and labour capacity as growth constraints for petty-commodity contractors. Two sets of findings were presented to address this question.

The findings show that: (i) petty-commodity builders use simple, general purpose tools and unskilled labour in the production of low-cost housing, (ii) capitalist production requires the use of specialized equipment as well as a skilled labour force to accomplish the specific tasks to be carried out in each stage of the construction process, (iii) petty-commodity producers have neither the financial means nor the socio-economic references necessary to acquire the equipment and to hire the labour force which is required in capitalist production, and (iv) access to this equipment and this labour force and the consequent movement of the builders towards capitalist production imply their loss of the ability to produce low-cost housing.

The findings confirm the correspondence presented in Tables 4.1 and 4.2 (between different forms of production, labour processes, and products which are necessary to the process of transformation of units of production). However, the findings also challenge some elements of this framework (without, however, invalidating it): (i) petty-commodity builders use a *majority*, not a *totality*, of simple, multi-purpose equipment and of unskilled labour in low-cost housing production, (ii) low-cost housing is not the only niche in petty-commodity production (also noted in the previous chapter) - and this niche reveals a way in which low-cost housing builders managed to change their activities, and (iii) not all the builders were willing to grow - thus, the argument under analysis should be rewritten to state that *the removal of the constraints on them will lead those petty-commodity producers who are willing to grow (and only them) to move towards capitalist production, and will drive them away from low-cost housing production.*

Considering the above reasoning, the model presented in Tables 4.1 and 4.2 is therefore modified, and is presented in amended form in Table 4.3.

As noted at different times in this chapter, access to equipment and labour capacity represent only a partial solution to the limitations to capitalize faced by petty-commodity builders. Other factors have to be taken into account as well. The following chapter examines two of these factors.

Table 4.3
Revised model of Tables 4.1 and 4.2: the continuum of production including form of production, labour process, product, equipment and labour capacity

labour	PCP	Handicraft
process	CP	Elementary manufacture
	ACP	Advanced manufacture to machinofacture
product	PCP	Low-cost housing and repair of higher cost buildings
	CP and ACP	Construction of complete higher cost buildings
equipment	PCP	Simple general purpose (for low-cost housing) and same set plus (mainly small-scale) specialized equipment (for other buildings)
	CP and ACP	Increasing predominance of specialized equipment
labour	PCP	Predominance of unskilled labour
capacity	CP	Increasing predominance of skilled labour
	ACP	Decrease in skills

Key:

PCP - petty-commodity production
CP   - capitalist production
ACP - advanced capitalist production

5 Constraints on growth:
Managerial capacity and credit

One of the two basic questions of this book was restated in the previous chapter in specific relation to equipment and labour capacity. It will be restated again here, in relation to the two factors being analyzed in this chapter. The particular question to be addressed here is the following: *What are the constraints on capitalization faced by petty-commodity builders in terms of obstacles to access to managerial capacity and credit, and how does their removal affect the participation of the builders in the provision of low-cost housing?*

Managerial capacity in petty-commodity and capitalist production

Lack of managerial capacity as a growth constraint is elaborated in this book in terms of the differences between the labour processes correspondent to petty-commodity and capitalist production. Petty-commodity producers, who use a handicraft process, do not have the managerial skills to carry out a manufacturing process. In handicraft, the master is directly involved in all stages of production. The workforce is constituted of apprentices and journeymen, who only help the master to carry out her/his work. Eventually a journeyman may be employed to carry out an independent task, but the managerial capacity that the master of the unit of production needs is minimal as compared with that required in manufacture. The type of management which exists in handicraft is conceptualized by Bonke and Goth as paternal management, which is based on the fact that master and labourers work together, and strong ties are developed between them (Bonke and Goth, 1983).

Division of labour is the basic characteristic which differentiates manufacture from handicraft (Chapter 2), and a directing authority over the labour force is essential in the former. This was noted, for instance, by Brewer, regarding production in general, and Goth, regarding construction (Brewer, 1984; Goth, 1984). In manufacture, the master of the production unit withdraws from direct production, delegating it to wage-labourers. The master - now a capitalist - has to assemble the workers in the workshop in a specific manner, according to the production process, and has to coordinate and

81

control their activities. The insertion of equipment and raw materials into the production process has also to be accurately planned and controlled (e.g. Goth, 1984). In manufacture, such operations are more intricate, due to their scale, than in handicraft. In the latter, the master operates a few simple tools directly to transform one or a few raw materials, and delivers just one product at a time. Machinofacture, which succeeds manufacture, also entails more complex, large-scale operations (Chapters 2 and 3), thus giving rise to a need for even greater management skills.

As Goth points out, there is a growth in the vertical division of labour, which accompanies the continuum of production (Goth, 1984). As the labour process becomes more complex, some managerial activities are delegated by the head of the unit of production to other professionals. This may alleviate the need for the managerial training of the head of the unit. However, the need for managerial training for the unit in general - head plus administrative team - increases. A conceptual model explaining the relationship between different forms of production, labour processes, and the products involved in the transformation of units of production was put forward in Chapter 2 (Table 2.2). It is now resumed in Table 5.1, with the inclusion of the changes in management.

Table 5.1
Conceptual model of the continuum of production including form of production, labour process, product and managerial capacity

labour	PCP	Handicraft
process	CP	Elementary manufacture
	ACP	Advanced manufacture to machinofacture
product	PCP	Low-cost housing
	CP and ACP	Other types of buildings
managerial	PCP	Paternal
capacity	CP and ACP	Increasing skills to meet the increasing complexity of production

Key:

PCP - petty-commodity production
CP - capitalist production
ACP - advanced capitalist production

The differences, in terms of managerial capacity, between petty-commodity and capitalist producers have been shown above. It is now important to understand why petty-commodity producers are constrained to acquire the managerial capacity necessary to establish capitalist production.

Without training opportunities to improve their managerial capacity, petty-commodity producers cannot grow. Such opportunities by and large exist in countries where capitalist production is prevalent. In these circumstances, it is unlikely that all the capitalist managers were trained abroad.

However, the existence of training programmes does not mean that they are easily accessible, for two reasons. Firstly, that there exists only restricted managerial training, which leave a large number of petty-commodity producers unattended. Secondly, that trainning exists, but petty-commodity producers cannot afford it. It is likely that both possibilities apply concurrently.

Although variations do occur depending on the country in question and the specific sector of the economy to which training is geared, in general terms educational facilities are limited throughout the developing world. At the same time, as noted in Chapter 2, petty-commodity producers face problems to save or accumulate. This leaves them ill equipped to meet extra costs such as those payable for managerial training.

Thus, it can be stated that petty-commodity builders are hindered from acquiring the managerial capacity necessary to establish capitalist production due to a combination of restricted availability of programmes and financial incapacity to pay for the existing programmes. This statement implies that informal means of achieving the managerial capacity necessary to establish capitalist production are also restricted - or else, lack of access to managerial capacity would not be a constraint on growth. It is acknowledged here that informal means of training are actually available throughout the developing world. However, they are not sufficient to raise an extensive number of petty-commodity producers to a point of becoming capitalist producers.

Assuming that petty-commodity producers have a drive to move towards capitalist production, if training is provided in order to enhance their managerial capacity, the possibility for growth will be open to them (obviously with a reminder that it is just a partial solution, once other constrains also need to be removed). However, as noted in the previous chapter, the capitalization of the builders implies the loss of their capacity to produce low-cost housing.

Credit in petty-commodity and capitalist production

The basic idea is that there is a differential between the level of credit required in petty-commodity and in capitalist production. Credit may be required to meet overheads and to acquire the factors of production (land, equipment, materials, labour, management) (e.g. Lipsey, 1971).

The need for credit in low-cost housing production in developing countries is negligible. Firstly, as already noted, the demand in low-income settlements is for contract, and not speculative building (Chapters 2 and 3). The provision of land and materials is not the builders' responsibility, but that of the clients. Thus petty-commodity builders have no need for credit for these factors.

The funds required to pay the workforce can be met by payments made by clients during the period of construction. Any remainder due would amount to a small sum. Since most labourers are unskilled and are engaged for short periods of time (Chapter 4), even the total sum required to pay them would not be weighty. Similarly, the equipment used by petty-commodity builders consists of simple tools, which do not require great expenditure - as compared with specialized tools and machines. The overheads of petty-commodity builders are irrelevant, as noted in Chapter 4, since they operate on an irregular and unregulated basis, spend nothing on items such as taxes, office apparatus and the like. Finally, their managerial capacity is very simple, as already noted. Its main requirement is a direct - paternal - interrelation with the labourers, rather than training to administer complex activities. So, considering these facts, there is no necessity for a significant expenditure on management either.

However, the credit requirements to establish capitalist production are different. As shown in Chapter 2, the evolution of the unit from handicraft to manufacture and machinofacture entails a growth in the complexity of the means and objects of production, which suggests the need for a larger volume of investment to establish capitalist production. This investment can be met either by accumulation and/or credit.

The role of accumulation in capitalist production was noted in Chapter 2. Capital is created and expands through a process of internal accumulation activated by production, defined by Marx as the circuit of capitalist production (Marx, 1977). However, as also noted, internal accumulation is not the only way to inject money at any given stage of the circuit of production. This may also take place through the provision of external credit from stocks of money that do not circulate.

Credit plays a role in the acceleration of the circuit of capital, and thus in the expanded reproduction of the capitalist system (e.g. Foley, 1986; Marx, 1977). This happens because the provision of credit substitutes and shortens a given period of accumulation of the money capital necessary to buy the commodities which will be used in production. As Foley suggests, the higher the sum of borrowing, the quicker the rate of expanded reproduction of capital. He also notes the role of credit in preventing insolvency and thus in maintaining the circuit of capitalist production (Foley, 1986).

There are a number of illustrations of the way in which credit has been used in the building industry, e.g. hiring of equipment, exchange deal with landowners, and the system of condominium. As noted in the previous chapter, the hire of equipment is a widespread practice. It constitutes a form of credit in allowing the hirer to acquire - albeight temporarily - some of the means of production. A form of credit used by speculative builders to acquire land is described by Beldecos in relation to Athens as the exchange deal. Builders exchange land with landowners in return for a number of housing units amongst the total to be built (Beldecos, 1987). Isik describes a similar procedure in Turkey. He also points out another form of credit, used by speculative builders to lessen the investment of their own capital in the acquisition of the different elements needed to carry out construction: the system of condominium, which consists of the sale of dwelling units before they are completed (Isik, 1992).

In short, the use of hired equipment, exchange deals and condominium systems reveals the existence of situations in which the circuit of production is fed by credit rather than by internal accumulation.

Monetary credit is also used in capitalist construction where units of production do not have enough capital and the above-mentioned forms of credit are unavailable. Also, if a new construction operation requires an increase in existing office apparatus to support it, an investment has to be made *before* the beginning of construction. Therefore, in both speculative and contract building, this investment cannot be carried out with the clients' money, which is disbursed only after or during the construction process. This money may come from the unit's own accumulation. However, since the circuit of capitalist production is not always a smooth process, and, as suggested by Foley, the unit may face periods of stagnation, credit assumes a vital role (Foley, 1986).

In sum, capitalist production requires credit to obtain the factors of production and meet those overheads which cannot be acquired through a process of internal accumulation. The idea of lack of access to credit as a growth constraint is supported by a number of authors who adopt the petty-commodity production approach. Gerry and Le Brun emphasise this constraint in their study of Dakar (Gerry, 1978; Le Brun and Gerry, 1975). A similar point is made by Scott in the context of Lima (Scott, 1979). Mautner focuses on housing specifically, noting how the lack of credit preempts the growth of petty-commodity builders in the periphery of São Paulo (Mautner, 1989). Gilbert points out not only the unavailability of credit to petty-commodity builders involved in low-cost housing production, but also the consequences of a policy of provision of credit. According to him, it is bound to induce capitalist penetration into this sector of the housing market (Gilbert, 1986).

It is important to identify the reasons for the lack of access to credit by petty-commodity producers which prevent them from establishing capitalist production. Following the same structure used previously, two main possibilities will be analyzed: unavailability of credit and lack of access to existing credit.

Similarly to the case of the preceding factors, the first possibility is not valid in countries where capitalist production takes place. However, the existence of credit does not mean that it is accessible to petty-commodity producers. The problems of access to equipment for hire have been noted in the previous chapter. The same reasoning applies for other forms of credit. Any agent who provides credit requires references from the potential borrower, since s/he wishes to ensure that the borrower is able to repay the money and the interest on it. Clients who enter into a system of condominium want a guarantee that the money that they pay to the builder will actually be invested in the construction of their housing units. Landowners who enter into an exchange deal want a guarantee that the builder has the capability to deliver a flat to him/her of the agreed standard. By and large, none of these requisites can be met by petty-commodity builders, since they are not registered units of production, have insufficient capital, no fixed income, and often lack even a formal address or proper personnal documents.

Thus, it can be stated that petty-commodity builders lack the socio-economic references to acquire the credit necessary to establish capitalist production. This implies that informal means of acquiring credit, such as family borrowing, are also restricted - otherwise, lack of access to credit in general would not be a problem.

As already shown, it is assumed here that petty-commodity producers have a drive to move towards capitalization. Thus, the provision of credit required to establish capitalist production would open up the possibility of growth, with the consequent withdrawal from low-cost housing production - bearing in mind that it is merely a fractional conclusion, since other factors must also be taken into account.

The conceptual model put forward in Table 2.2 is now resumed in Table 5.2, in order to take into account the effect of credit.

Table 5.2
Conceptual model of the continuum of production including form of production, labour process, product and credit

labour	PCP	Handicraft
process	CP	Elementary manufacture
	ACP	Advanced manufacture to machinofacture
product	PCP	Low-cost housing
	CP and ACP	Other types of buildings
credit	PCP	Negligible
	CP and ACP	To counteract phases of lack of internal accumulation

Key:

PCP - petty-commodity production
CP   - capitalist production
ACP - advanced capitalist production

The growth constraints faced by petty-commodity producers due to their lack of access to managerial capacity and credit have now been analyzed. The argument developed so far shows that: (i) petty-commodity builders use a paternal system of management in the production of low-cost housing, and the credit required to carry out this production is negligible, (ii) capitalist production requires credit to obtain the factors of production and to meet overheads which cannot be paid for as the result of a process of internal accumulation, and at the same time requires managerial capacity which includes a directing authority over the labour force to guide its organization in a specific manner according to the production process, as well as to guide the planning and control of the insertion of equipment and raw materials into the production process, at a more complex scale than in petty-commodity production, (iii) petty-commodity builders do not have the socio-economic references to acquire the credit necessary to establish capitalist production and at the same time are hindered from acquiring the necessary managerial capacity due to a combination of restricted training facilities and their financial incapacity to pay for the training, and (iv) the provision of the credit and the managerial capacity necessary to establish capitalist production and the consequent movement of builders along the continuum towards capitalist production imply their loss of the ability to produce low-cost housing in developing countries.

The builders

Now, findings related to managerial capacity and credit gathered from the activities of the builders introduced in the previous chapters will be presented. Managerial capacity and credit will be analyzed consecutively.

Managerial capacity

Managerial capacity for low-cost housing production The duties of builders engaged in low-cost housing construction are evidenced in the following statement given by the exclusive builder Alberto:

> All my work is building for the poor, as I told you... I undertake many different types of work, depending on the characteristics of the house, and the stage of the construction process... However, in terms of the work which is not construction itself, if you like, it does not vary much... I have to calculate the quantity and the type of materials which the client has to buy, calculate how many days my work will take, how many people I have to hire, and how much I will charge for my work and to pay my men... I also have to hire my apprentices, generally one or two boys to help me with basic work such as carrying materials, or mixing concrete... Eventually I hire a journeyman, if the client is in a hurry to get the service done, and can afford to pay me and the journeyman at the same time... The process of hiring the guys is very simple... It is just one or two or three people, who are easy to find through my personal contacts; and there are no papers to sign, just agreement by word... I am always working side-by-side with my workers, therefore I have no difficulty in controlling them. And the intimacy that we share helps the work. A good atmosphere is very important.

Most of Alberto's work relates to his direct involvement in the production process. As shown, he has very few managerial tasks in his production of low-cost housing. His is a paternal form of management, entailing close ties between master and assistants. The other builders who produce low-cost housing, belonging to the exclusive, mixed and hybrid groups, have slight variations in the number of personnel hired, ranging from nought to five. However, all these builders have a managerial role similar to that of Alberto in their work in low-income settlements.

Managerial capacity for other activities This section shows that the managerial capacity necessary in capitalist production includes (i) a directing authority over the labour force, (ii) its organization in a specific manner according to the production process, as well as (iii) the planning and control of the insertion of equipment and raw materials in the production process, on a more complex level than in petty-commodity production.

As already noted, the analysis of builders who work outside low-income settlements revealed three main types of activity: the repair and maintenance of middle- and high-cost housing, the construction of complete single housing units or other types of buildings, and the construction of several housing units and/or other types of buildings concomitantly. Each type requires a more complex managerial capacity than the previous one.

An illustration of the skills required to undertake the repair and maintenance of middle- and high-cost housing is given by the mixed builder Tomas:

> When I carry out repairs for middle- and high-income families, I have to handle the building materials, which is something that a builder normally does not do in a low-income area... The rich pay us more for our services, and, in exchange, they do not want to get involved or to worry about construction... We have to deal with the building materials, which means a strict control on the flow of money between myself and the dealer of the materials and between the client and me, because one can lose a lot with inflation... It is not that I have to pay the increase in price from my pocket, but, imagine what the client thinks if he has to disburse more because I was caught by inflation! He will blame me, will not call me for another job.

The other mixed builder, Dorcelino, and the transitional builder, Elisio, carry out the same type of work, and need a similar level of managerial capacity. This work, although also carried out using a petty-commodity form of production, is more complex in managerial terms than the construction of low-cost housing, due to the handling of materials.

The construction of complete houses using a capitalist form of production requires further managerial skills. The hybrid builder Rafael, for example, stated the following:

> On a building contract I need labourers, materials, tools, sometimes machines, and I have to plan their insertion into the production process as precisely as possible... If I do not have the right labourers, equipment and materials at the right time, I have to stop the construction, and lose money. The client does not pay me to be still... If I hire a machine, for example, and the labourer to operate it is not there, or if the materials do not arrive on time, I lose money... If the labourers are there and the machines or materials do not arrive, I lose money as well... On top of that, there is inflation, which makes my task of controlling the cash more difficult.

The semi-capitalist builder Joaquim also mentions the handling of design as another factor which differentiates the construction of low-cost housing from that of complete dwellings for the middle- and high-income classes:

> In low-income areas, the client sometimes comes to me with a plan for his house given by a state agency, or copied from some acquaintance. But most of the time they ask me to draw the plan myself... At any rate, they are very simple designs, and do not require any contact with architects or engineers... But the larger the house, the more complicated the matter gets. Some middle-income clients want a proper and specific design for their houses, not just a sketch made by me, or a plan provided by a state agency... So, sometimes, in order to help them, I hire a draughtsman, and then find an engineer or architect to sign and be responsible for the design... Other clients give me a plan designed by an architect, and in this case, I have to come to

an agreement with the architect, in order to monitor the execution of the design properly... And the more complex the building, the more complicated the design: you might need structural plans, water and sewage plans, electrical plans, sometimes fire, air-conditioning and telephone systems... And the more complex the plans, the more complex the monitoring.

The cases of the other hybrid builders replicate those of Rafael and Joaquim regarding the complexity of operations. An account of the type of estimation required on a larger commission in comparison to that required in low-cost housing production is given by the exclusive builder Amin:

> I give prices per day of work, which is simpler than per square meter [of built work]... If you give the price per square meter, you have to know the quantity of man-hours required for each unit of area, and, starting from there, you then calculate the total price... But I know by heart how long I take to carry out each construction work, and it is easier for me to give a price by estimating how many days each work takes... I acknowledge that the larger the contract, the more difficult it is to price it per day... But I do not take large contracts anyway... They are too troublesome for me.

The method of pricing used by Amin is also used by the other exclusive builders. It is imprecise, because the builders have only a loose estimate of the number of days which will be necessary to carry out a given contract, simply based on their previous experiences, of which they have no written record. The cases of the exclusive builders show that this method limits them, because they cannot take larger contracts without an accurate calculation of all the elements involved.

The managerial skills specifically related to handling the labour force are illustrated by the following statement given by the hybrid builder Baltazar:

> I have built many finished dwellings, which require more administration than my work in low-income settlements... To begin with, you have to handle a larger number of workers... For example, for that house that I have just completed, which is approximately 120 square meters; as far as I remember I first employed one carpenter with an apprentice, one reinforcement fixer with an apprentice, and one bricklayer with three apprentices for the foundations and structure... For the walls and panelling I needed one painter and two bricklayers, each one with one apprentice... For the roofing, I needed two carpenters and their apprentices... For plastering, one plasterer, one tile setter, one bricklayer, and four apprentices... For the doors and windows, one carpenter, one jointer, one bricklayer, and their apprentices... For the flooring, one wood and one ceramic floor fixer, one carpenter, one bricklayer and their apprentices... For plumbing and electrical installations, one plumber, one electrician, one bricklayer and their apprentices... For painting and finishing, one painter, two bricklayers and one apprentice for each one of them... I had between four and eight people at the same time under my supervision on the site, whereas in low-income areas

I have one or two, rarely, a third one... When I have got more than one contract to build complete houses at the same time, I have had to put a foreman on each site which had more than five or six labourers [working on it]. The larger the number of labourers, the more complex it is to handle them.

Apart from the quantitative aspect of the labour force, Baltazar also mentioned the qualitative aspects:

I am the one who does most of the building work in poor dwellings... My few workers just help me there, and it is very easy to control them, because their tasks are so simple, and I am with them most of the time... In the case of the complete house that I was talking about, all the construction work is carried out by labourers, therefore my task in terms of supervision to secure high quality of work is greater... The management of the workforce also requires a great deal of bureaucracy, because I have to register each labourer, pay a percentage of his wages to the INPS [social security], deposit another percentage for his guarantee fund, and, when I need to fire someone, a whole scheme has to be set up, to release the guarantee fund, pay compensation, and so on. There is a lot of red tape. But with my own apprentices and journeymen, it is just cash-in-hand.

Thus, Baltazar's illustrations show the complexity of his managerial tasks in a manufacture process, as opposed to handicraft. There are slight variations in the size and composition of the workforce of the semi-capitalist and the other hybrid builders compared to that of Baltazar, but all of them have experienced similar bureaucratic procedures as regards hiring, maintenance and dismissal of labourers. Their cases replicate that of Baltazar regarding the management of the workforce.

The cases of all the exclusive builders show that there is a strong personal contact between them and their labourers. If the scale of their labour force increases, either due to a large scale contract or a series of small-scale ones, the intimate association loosens, and is not replaced by a proper management structure. This finding reveals that, even if labour capacity is provided to the builders in the way shown in the previous chapter, they will not utilize it, if appropriate managerial training is not provided.

The bureaucracy faced by builders to build complete houses is not limited to the regulation of the labour force, but includes the regulation of the construction itself, as mentioned in Chapter 3. Thus, builders need the skills to liaise with the CREA (the authority which controls the proper administration of construction), as well as with the municipal authority both during and after construction is completed.

Capitalist and advanced capitalist builders need managerial skills to build several residential units concomitantly. Like semi-capitalist and hybrid builders, they also need managerial skills to deal with equipment, materials, the workforce, the integration of these elements, and the bureaucracy relating to the construction operations.

The concomitant construction of several complete dwellings also require greater off-site activities in terms of planning and administration. As the advanced capitalist Gustavo puts it:

> When I built one house at a time, I used to do all the personnel and financial work. But in order to build these apartment blocks, I need staff to deal specifically with these matters... The office workload increases, and, even if I delegate functions to someone else, my managerial workload increases as well, because now I have to monitor the work of more people, apart from the fact that part of the office work is still under my direct responsibility.

Gustavo and Gastão, operating as speculative builders, have additional managerial duties related to the advertisement and the sale of housing units.

In short, the findings show the complexity of the managerial capacity required in the work carried out using a capitalist form of production. Next, the constraints that petty-commodity builders have to acquire the managerial capacity to establish capitalist production will be analyzed.

The process of acquisition of managerial capacity As already noted, the managerial capacity required for low-cost housing production is simple. Accordingly, builders did not have problems in acquiring it. As shown in Chapters 3 and 4, a number of builders were first trained as wage-labourers in a registered building unit of production, and later expanded their skills through on-the-job training as independent builders. A second set of builders was trained in domestic units of production, run by their fathers. Both sets acquired not only the labour skills but also the managerial skills necessary to produce low-cost housing. However, the acquisition of the managerial capacity required for capitalist production presented problems. The exclusive builder Juvenal, for instance, stated

> To set up the firm I want to, I do need more training, but there is no way of getting it now... There are not many ways of getting training... I would have liked to go to the university and become an engineer, as a dream, but I do not have enough schooling... There are the technical schools, yes, like the SENAI [Industrial Educational Scheme], professional training, but still, there are not many of them... Another problem with the SENAI is that they give preference to people sent by a building firm. The boss of the firm where I work part-time as a labourer [in parallel to his independent work as a low-cost housing builder] will only send me if he thinks that my training will be helpful to him, he will not send me just to help me establishing myself as an independent builder... I thought about enroling at the SENAI, but, you know, even without considering money matters and even if I get a place, I do not know how to fit it into my day-to-day life, because I work during the week as a bricklayer, and have to travel almost two hours to work. Now I am working in [the neighbourhood of] Santa Efigenia, and it means almost another hour from the construction site to the SENAI, door-to-door... Then I also need to travel back home after the course late at night, and be up again the next day

at four... The other alternative is to get on-the-job training as a foreman, but it does not depend only on me, there are not enough places... I think I am a good bricklayer, but I have colleagues who work with me that are good as well, and if the boss needs a new foreman, only one of us will be chosen... Then what happens to the others? There are just not enough places.

Exclusive builders also face financial problems to acquire training. Ronan, for instance suggested:

> To get a place in the SENAI, I need at least to complete the fourth year of schooling, and I just have one... And to go back to school, even if I can get a place, I do not know how I would manage in terms of money... It is difficult for me to pay for the schooling of my children, and they come first. Imagine having to pay for the schooling of an extra child, that is, me!

There are indeed some possibilities of free schooling for adults. However, the places are, once again, limited. Besides, Ronan's financial situation prevents his access to a course in another way:

> With the problems that I am facing with my family, I have to work as much as I can... It is not fun to work as a labourer during the week, and then work as a builder in my spare time. I do it because I have no alternative... I have to work as much as I can, to give the minimum to my children and wife... Then I cannot attend training, can I?... Even in the periods when I do not have much work, I could not be in a class room. I have to be looking for a job, I have to show myself to be available. No one will look for me in a class room.

A solution to this problem would be to combine training and income-generation. However, this leads to the previous problem:

> If I could get a place as a foreman, this problem would be solved... I get paid, and I learn... It may happen, one day, but it may as well not happen... Find me a bricklayer who does not want to be a foreman! But there are not many vacancies as foreman, right? Many bricklayers will continue to be bricklayers.

The problems faced by Ronan are replicated in the case of the other exclusive builders. In short, this group of builders does not have access to the training necessary to acquire managerial capitalist capacity due to a combination of four factors: restricted access to training facilities, the distant location of existing facilities, the financial difficulties regarding payment for this course, and the need to use the time which would to be spent on training for income-generation.

The difficulties of obtaining managerial capacity are also illustrated by the cases of those builders working outside low-income settlements. First, the acquisition of the capacity necessary to carry out the repair and maintenance of middle- and high-cost housing will be presented. Next, the acquisition of the capacity to produce complete dwellings or other types of building will be presented.

Mixed and transitional builders acquired some of the managerial capacity required for repair and maintenance before starting to work as independent builders. The rest was acquired after having started working outside low-income settlements. The mixed builder Tomas, for example, gave the following statement in relation to the acquisition of skills necessary for the handling of the purchase of building materials during periods of high inflation in the country:

> A few years ago, when inflation was low, it was not difficult to administer the purchase of materials... But as inflation soared, many builders gave up. I decided to act differently... My experience in times of low inflation gave me the knowledge of how to handle the cash flow regarding materials... Then, when inflation started to creep up, I already had a basic knowledge of how do deal with cash flow. But I also had the chance of going to elementary school until the fourth year, and later on I did a technical course in architectural draughtsmanship. I wanted to become an architect, you know... None of these courses gave me specific knowledge of financial management, but they gave me a basic ability to reason and [knowledge of] mathematics. The rest was [due to] my own courage in facing the practical problems and my efforts to develop from this basis, and apply my knowledge of accountancy... My experience in repair and maintenance for middle-income families was essential, very important to consolidate this knowledge... In the beginning it was a sort of on-the-job training, because I was still absorbing experience. But soon I picked it up... I could not apply it in low-income neighbourhoods, there is no need for accounting gimmicks there.

As shown before, the acquisition of the above skill is crucial to enable a low-cost housing builder to engage in the repair and maintenance of middle- and high-cost housing. The other mixed builder and the transitional builder, Dorcelino and Elisio, have a similar case.

As the preceding chapter demonstrates, the specialized equipment and labour capacity necessary to carry out work outside low-income settlements were acquired after builders start working in the repair and maintenance of middle- and high-cost housing (with the rare exception of those builders who inherited a number of tools from their fathers). The situation regarding managerial capacity is different, because, as the examples of the transitional and mixed builders show, some of the fundamental skills were acquired even before they start working as independent builders in low-income settlements. The cases of the hybrid, semi-capitalist, capitalist and advanced capitalist builders, to be presented shortly, confirm this pattern. At any rate, it is important to note that none of the skills were acquired *during* the period of full-time work in low-income settlements. The problems faced by the exclusive builders, presented before, were also faced by the other builders when they were in a similar stage.

Hybrid, semi-capitalist, capitalist and advanced capitalist builders acquired the managerial capacity necessary to build complete houses from different sources:

training as foremen, training with their fathers, schooling, or on-the-job training. These sources were combined differently in each case.

Augusto, Waldemar and Rafael learned their basic skills from their fathers. Augusto and Waldemar did not even finish the first year of elementary school, while Rafael reinforced his skills by attending until the fourth year.

The case of the remaining builders is different. The most important element in their learning process was their training as foremen, before they started working as independent builders. This training was supplemented with schooling and on-the-job learning.

Baltazar, Joaquim, Wander and Gastão supplemented their schooling after starting work in the repair and maintenance of middle- and high-cost housing. Their experience is illustrated by the following testimony given by Baltazar:

> I owe a lot to Mr. Wagner, the engineer who promoted me to the post of foreman. I worked very close to him, and absorbed his knowledge of how to conduct the construction of a complete house... During my period of work with Mr. Wagner, I was able to learn how to control the labour force, hire equipment, buy materials, and connect these things together... But specially the paperwork and financial calculations were particularly difficult to grasp. I realized that I would learn more if I invested in my schooling. At that time I did not have means to resume schooling, nor when I was working only in low-income neighbourhoods... But after establishing myself a bit better financially, I went to attend four more years of school at night, and this really enabled me to grasp the parts of the construction business related to paperwork and financial calculations. Then it was a matter of practising, and learning from my own practice. With resolution and courage... It took me a lot of effort, and I am proud of it.

José and Gustavo had a better school training before commencing work as foremen - attending until the fifth and sixth year. They did not go back to school later. However, on-the-job training in the repair and maintenance of middle- and high-cost housing was regarded by them as an important step in the consolidation of their learning process. Jorge also went through a similar process of acquisition of skills.

The principal conclusion to be drawn from the findings presented in this section is that none of the builders have been able to acquire the capacity required to establish capitalist production while working full-time in the construction of low-cost housing. The following section will explain the effects of the acquisition of this capacity.

The effects of developing managerial capacity As in the case of equipment and labour capacity, the effects of the acquisition of managerial capacity will be analyzed through policy-like situations and scenarios.

As noted before, the mixed and transitional builders need managerial skills to deal with the building materials in order to carry out the repair and maintenance of middle- and high-cost housing. However, this work leads to an increase in their fees, a fact which damages their ability to produce low-cost housing (Chapter 3). Semi-capitalist and hybrid builders have shifted fractionally from petty-commodity to capitalist production, while capitalist and advanced capitalist builders have shifted totally. This process was initially limited by lack of managerial capacity. The builders had acquired the basis of this capacity beforehand, but they had to complement it with subsequent schooling and/or on-the-job training afterwards. In order to do so, they had to find places in the restricted school system, and also obtain work in the repair and maintenance of middle- and high-cost housing, which would provide them with the practical training they needed. Their work outside low-income settlements, in turn, provided them with the financial means to enrol in further education.

So, the subsequent acquisition of managerial skills enabled the builders to set up capitalist production. However, as demonstrated in Chapters 3 and 4, this led to the loss of characteristics which are essential for the production of low-cost housing. Testimonies given by the builders, presented earlier, reveal that they moved away from low-cost housing production. They now need specialized managerial skills, to set up manufacture production. However, this production acquires rigidity and costs which are appropriate to large-scale production. The establishment of this process thus leaves the builders unable to operate in a flexible manner and for a price low enough to meet the needs of low-income settlements.

Semi-capitalist and hybrid builders lose the capacity to produce low-cost housing while they are building complete houses elsewhere. Their managerial skills encourages them to leave low-income settlements whenever possible. Joaquim, the semi-capitalist builder, has already left those settlements entirely, because he has sufficient demand for the repair and maintenance of middle- and high-cost housing when he is not building complete residences. Capitalist and advanced capitalist builders, who have a continuous demand for the construction of complete houses, were found to have lost the capacity to produce low-cost housing completely.

In summary, the cases of those builders who abandon the production of low-cost housing either partially or totally reveal the possible effect of a policy which would replace the current process of acquisition of managerial capacity necessary to establish capitalist production.

The scenarios constructed on the basis of plans made by builders who currently produce low-cost housing will now be examined. Like the cases of equipment and labour capacity, the possibility of provision of managerial capacity attracted a number of the builders, but not all of them. Those who welcomed the suggestion were the exclusive builders Juvenal, Evandro and Ronan, and the hybrid builder Rafael.

Juvenal, Evandro and Ronan recognized the need for further training in order to upgrade their units of production. Rafael already had a thorough knowledge of construction management, but had no training as to the financial aspects of management necessary to establish the speculative building operations which he was planning. The possibilities discussed with the builders centred on the two principal limitations on their access to managerial capacity: restricted access to training schemes, and their financial situation. A statement given by Evandro is a good illustration of the response obtained from builders who want to upgrade themselves:

> More training courses sure help, there is no doubt about it... Something in the Agua Branca [the neighbourhood where he lives]. For example, I would pop in after work, that would be nice... At least I would not have to bother to

find a course, or to travel back and forth... We already discussed why I cannot pay for a course now. If I get a loan, that is fine, but I still have the problem of time... A loan for buying equipment or for hiring labour makes more sense, I think, because I can continue working the number of hours that I do now, or even more. But a loan to pay for the course is complicated, because I would be using the money in the first instance to work less hours.

The willingness to accept loans for equipment and labour but not for managerial capacity seemed problematic, because the first two factors could not be used without the third. Confronted with this situation, Evandro responded:

I know that, if I do not invest in my own training, there is no sense in buying equipment, or hiring more people. This is a problem which needs to be sorted out... I know that, with training, in the future I would be more qualified, but no one knows about the future, it is a risk... The problem of working hours is complicated, really. I need as much time as I can to work... If the course is free, like in the SENAI, it is better, of course, but I still do not know how to compensate for the hours I would be sitting in class.

The possible solutions to these problems, which came out of the discussion with Evandro were the following:

The ideal thing would be a scheme similar to on-the-job training to become a foreman. You learn, but you also earn... If the government is really willing to help, it would be necessary to set up a sort of grant scheme for attending the courses. So, while I learn, I am not working, but at least my children will be eating... One possibility would be to introduce a course in my neighbourhood, and just a few hours a week, very slowly... It would need to be close to my home in order to maintain the contact with the people here. If I disappear, there will be no work for me... It is important that people feel that I am around, that I am easily accessible. If I am away for a few hours per week, and attending a course in the neighbourhood, the guys can reach me at any time. But not if I go to SENAI, for example, and come home late at night... To go to the SENAI, I would need support, to compensate for the work I would be losing.

The scenarios with Juvenal, Ronan and Rafael replicate that of Evandro. In short, the most viable proposal seems to be the provision of access to a training scheme in the vicinity in which builders live. An alternative solution could be the access to training elsewhere, but backed by a grant scheme. Nevertheless, the scenarios envisaged by these builders show that, if feasible support programmes are implemented, a departure from low-cost housing production would occur. The cases of those builders who were unwilling to undertake managerial training will now be examined.

As noted in the previous chapter, Alberto, Amin and Waldemar were willing to engage in wage-work. João Pedro, Dorcelino, Tomas and Baltazar wanted to continue their current activities. None of these builders changed their plans when presented

96

with the possibility of access to managerial training. Similarly, the possibility of providing appropriate managerial capacity to establish a few small-scale teams to expand their production of low-cost housing - and their income - did not change their plans. This idea did not interest the other builders either.

The case of Augusto and Rafael is distinct from that of the previous builders because they were willing to upgrade their businesses: to set up one unit specializing in hydraulic and electrical services, and to become a speculative builder/landowner respectively. However, both already possessed the skills to put such plans into action, and were therefore not interested in training schemes.

The above information concludes the findings regarding the connection between access to managerial capacity and the production of low-cost housing by petty-commodity builders. The policy-like situations of those builders operating a capitalist form of production and the scenarios of those builders who are willing to accept the provision of further managerial capacity confirm the reasoning about the movement of the builders towards capitalist production and their departure from low-income settlements. Like in the case of equipment and labour capacity, the scenarios envisaged here reveal that a number of builders do not want to improve their managerial capacity. However, considering that provision of managerial capacity does not affect some builders, but leads others away from low-income settlements, the general result is a decline in the participation of builders in the supply of low-cost housing.

The next section presents data about the last element analyzed in this book.

Credit

Credit for low-cost housing production The following analysis is divided according to the six factors elaborated in the theoretical analysis about credit (presented earlier in this chapter): land, building materials, labour, equipment, overheads and managerial capacity.

The findings about the first factor reveal that there are variations in the methods of acquisition of land in different types of low-income settlement - i.e. from formal acquisition totally regulated by local authorities to illegal invasion. However, the contract builders do not need to buy land in order to build low-cost housing and therefore do not need credit to acquire it.

In relation to building materials, three situations were found to exist as regards their acquisition: purchase by clients prior to the hire of a builder, purchase by clients during the period of construction, and provision by the state. The following testimony given by the exclusive builder Evandro epitomizes the first situation:

> Some of my clients managed to save enough money to buy the building materials for the construction work that they wish to be carried out in their homes... After having bought and stored the material, they start saving again in order to hire me to carry out the work... In order to buy the right types and quantities of materials, some of these clients seek advice from an acquaintance with skills in the construction industry, or from a building materials shop; and when they hire me, the material is all there... Other clients make contact with me initially so that I can advise them to purchase

the materials; then they would call me some time later after having saved enough to pay my services.

The second situation is illustrated by the following statement given by the mixed builder Tomas:

> Some people manage to save enough money to pay for the building materials and my services at the same time. This depends of course on the extend of the construction work which they require... It usually happens when they change jobs, and receive compensation for being fired from the former one... In this scheme, the client hires me, I estimate the materials necessary for the job, then he buys them either altogether at the beginning of construction, usually when the work is small, or buys them bit-by-bit according to the progress of the construction process... In any case, I have never advanced my own money to purchase materials, nor sought credit to do it.

The third situation occurs in the sites-and-services settlements. The clients receive the materials from the state, therefore the builder is not involved in their purchase.

All the builders studied faced one or several of the above situations. In short, as in the case of land, none of them needed to purchase materials to produce low-cost housing. Consequently, they never required credit for this purpose. However, their contract building work in low-income settlements did include expenditures with other factors, which will be examined next.

The need for labour was examined in the previous chapter, and the main points will be recapitulated here. Two basic situations have been encountered. Firstly, builders who have managed to save and form a reserve fund to pay their workforce in the event of a delay in payment by the client. Secondly, builders who have not managed to save, and therefore work alone or hire assistants only when there is sufficient evidence that the clients will pay them without postponement.

The first group of builders needed a fund to pay, at the maximum, two apprentices and one journeyman for a period of two weeks. According to them, this was not a large sum. Besides, it could be saved little-by-little, because their penetration in the low-income market was gradual - i.e. the fund increased with the demand.

It could be argued that the builders on the second group needed a credit facility, for they had not been able to save. However, even without savings or credit, they managed to produce low-cost housing for a certain portion of the low-income population.

The requirements in terms of equipment to produce low-cost housing also have been examined in the preceding chapter. Two main situations were identified. Firstly, builders who started their careers as trainees in a craft office in a registered construction unit, and thus had to acquire a basic set of tools during the initial period of instruction. This was an indispensable condition to be upgraded to the post of official. The acquisition of this equipment was not difficult. In order to work independently in low-income settlements, they had to acquire other tools related to their initial crafts as well as to other crafts. However, the acquisition of this second set was not problematic either, since the tools were cheap, and were acquired bit-by-bit over a period of two to four years. The builders bought their tools using their own savings, without need for credit. The second situation included the builders who inherited most of their equipment from their fathers, and merely supplemented their sets with occasional purchases paid for with their savings. These builders did not therefore require credit either.

The requirements in terms of overheads to produce low-cost housing were analyzed in Chapter 3. It was shown that the only two costs that builders had incurred other than those specifically related to production were transport and their own social security. Transport costs arise when a builder works at a distance from his neighbourhood. According to the builders interviewed, this seldom happens, and, when it does, the cost is minimal, corresponding only to a tiny fraction of the daily fee charged by the builder.

The managerial capacity required to produce low-cost housing was analyzed in the present chapter. As shown, this capacity was low, and was acquired either through training in a registered construction unit, or with the builder's father, in a domestic unit. Credit was not necessary.

In short, the need for credit required for the production of low-cost housing through contract was negligible. However, as will be shown next, this situation changed as the builders moved away from low-income settlements.

Credit for other activities As previously, the need for credit in relation to land, materials, labour, equipment, overheads and managerial capacity will be considered consecutively. Only the advanced capitalist builders Gustavo and Gastão have dealt with the purchase of land. This is because they build speculatively. Gustavo's experience is the following:

> I am a developer now, and, unlike in contract building, I cannot rely on clients' capital to acquire land... Land is expensive, and in order to go from contract building to become a developer, I used to make deals with landowners. Instead of buying their plots of land, I would first build a block of flats on each one, and then give them the number of flats equivalent to the price of each plot. By doing this, I have avoided the need to advance my own capital, which I did not have at that time, to buy land... However, such deals are getting scarce nowadays. I build mostly for lower middle-income people, in neighbourhoods out of Belo Horizonte's central area, and landowners are not willing to take apartments in such neighbourhoods. They think that their price will not rise, and they cannot get high rents... Therefore, now I have to invest my own capital to purchase land, which amounts to approximately 10% of the cost of each building... In order to buy a plot of land, sometimes I use my own capital alone, or combine it with that of a friend... This friend is just willing to invest in the construction along with me, and share the profits.

The situation in relation to building materials is similar to that of land. Only the advanced capitalist builders have dealt with its purchase. The detachment of other builders from materials is illustrated by the following statement given by Joaquim:

The basic agreement between myself and a client is that he will pay me every week, and then I use this money to sort out all the needs to continue the construction in the following week. But this ideal situation does not happen all the time, because maybe the client is dependent on a loan, which may be delayed, or has an emergency, or something like that... Then I am prepared to back the construction for the following week, in order not to stop it. I would lose a lot if I stopped it and then began again, you know... The only thing that I really do not like to get involved with is materials. Their price is so erratic, you know, inflation and all the rest... I need to see that the client is committed to solving all the problems regarding the price of the materials, and the best commitment possible is the spending of his own money... If the client has to delay payment for the materials, we can go together and make a deal with the dealer, in order to postpone the invoice. That can be done... What I do not do is to pay from my own pocket.

The situation of the advanced capitalist builders is, however, different. Gastão has records of figures relating to some of his previous developments, which, adjusted to values current at the time of fieldwork, show that he spent Cr$675,000.00 on materials for each residential unit of a complex of eight semi-detached 60 square meters two bedroom units, Cr$727,944.00 on each flat in a block of eight 60 square meters two bedroom flats, Cr$716,192.00 on each residential unit in a complex of eight semi-detached 80 square meters three bedroom units, and Cr$798,408.00 on each flat in a block of eight 80 square meters three bedroom flats. The capital for these activities was acquired through his own savings and from acquaintances willing to invest in his business.

Gustavo acquired the materials for his developments through two main schemes. Firstly, deals made with distributors whereby they would provide building materials in exchange for a given number of residential units to be handed over on completion of the building work. Secondly, the system of condominium, whereby Gustavo negotiated the selling of residential units to clients during the construction of the building, and used their capital to accomplish it. Gustavo also has invested his own capital in some of his previous developments. Nevertheless, both he and Gastão could not count only on their own capital in order to acquire building materials. They also had to rely on different schemes of credit.

In contrast to the situation regarding land and materials, the need for credit in order to pay the workforce also affected those builders working on a contracting scheme. As shown in the previous chapter, mixed and transitional builders did not encounter problems in hiring the labour force required for the repair and maintenance of middle- and high-cost housing. However, the case of the builders involved in the production of complete dwellings is different. Hybrid, semi-capitalist and capitalist builders needed a reserve fund to guard against delays by clients in paying the workforce.

According to Baltazar, Augusto, Waldemar and Joaquim, on some occasions they were contracted to carry out a construction service, but had insufficient equipment or labourers, as well as insufficient savings to obtain them. Under these circumstances, they relied on hired equipment, and on loans to pay hired labourers. The following statement given by Joaquim describes the situation well:

Unfortunately, it is impossible to predict the evolution of my business, it depends on so many things... The way the country as a whole is going, government actions, the particular income situation of my clients, whether I am able to get more clients or not, many things... My reserve fund also depends on many things. Most of the time I manage to save a little, but it does not mean that this money is going to the bank, and will stay there. One has so many necessities, you know... One month everything might be O.K. at home, so I save more. But the following month a kid might get sick, or I need to buy materials to repair part of my own house, or my wife pressures me to buy something new, whatever. Then the money goes there... Or I might need to replace a tool, or to buy a new one... No matter how much you plan these things, there are always surprises.

The above quotation illustrates the fluctuations both in demand, and in extent of the funds in reserve. Depending on the level of each of these two variables at a given point, the funds might not be enough to meet the requirements of the demand.

Rafael was the only hybrid builder who did not need credit from acquaintances in order to hire labourers. This was due to his ability to manage his savings, a lesser personal and household expenditure (he had only one child, as compared to the other builders questioned who had several), and his workforce was smaller. However, as will be shown later, Rafael required credit for other items.

The capitalist builders were in a more complex situation than that of the hybrid and semi-capitalist builders. They built several complete houses simultaneously, which require a larger workforce and are subject to the same uncertainties in terms of reserve funds as Baltazar, Waldemar and Joaquim. Thus, they too had to rely on occasional borrowing.

Gastão and Gustavo, in their turn, incurred greater expenses in terms of labour than the hybrid, semi-capitalist and capitalist builders. Being speculative builders, they had to seek funds to pay all the workforce necessary to carry out each development. Gastão sought investments from acquaintances to meet such costs, while Gustavo used the same method, as well as the system of condominium.

Similarly to the case of labour, the need for credit for equipment was present among both the contract and the speculative builders. However, as already noted, these builders did not use financial credit from acquaintances, but hired the equipment.

The issue of equipment already appeared in the presentation of the data about credit for the workforce. A parallel was made about the need to hire equipment and the need to borrow money to pay labourers. As shown in the preceding chapter, the builders who carry out the construction of complete houses hired equipment at some point in the development of their units of production, and/or still do it.

The need for credit to meet overheads will be analyzed now. As shown in Chapter 3, mixed and transitional builders are able to meet the overheads involved in the repair and maintenance of middle- and high-cost housing. However, the case of those builders engaged in the construction of complete dwellings differs. It has been shown that the basic problems suffered by hybrid and semi-capitalist builders relate to taxes, transportation, and the fees payable to an engineer to be legally responsible for the site. These are not considered as labour costs because, for instance, the engineer is not directly involved in production. The builders do not have official qualifications and therefore need someone with a degree to be the 'frontman' for the construction. Of the hybrid and the semi-capitalist builders, Baltazar, Rafael and Joaquim did not need credit to meet the above expenses, but relied on advance payments from clients and their own savings. However, Augusto and Waldemar encountered problems, especially with regard to the engineer. A statement given by Waldemar is a good illustration of the situation:

> These engineers are mean, you know. Just because they have a diploma, they come and charge a lot to put their names on the construction... It is generally 1% of the estimated costs of the construction, but some charge even more than that, 2%... The engineer who signs the papers for me now is O.K., we manage to do all right financially. But I had a problem some years ago, because I found an engineer who told me: 'listen, what we are doing is illegal, and I am not going to stick my neck out without a guarantee'; so I had to pay him beforehand. But I could not tell this to the client and ask for money; I had to pretend that everything was fine, under control... All I did was to borrow from a friend.

Capitalist builders have the same expenses as those of hybrids' and semi-capitalists', plus the fees of a bookkeeper, which are approximately Cr$500.00 per hour. Both builders in this group had problems in meeting their overheads in the past, and relied on borrowing from acquaintances.

The advanced capitalist builders had even greater overheads, because both had registered building units and a permanent head office and therefore expenses such as office personnel, rent, telephone and electricity bills, photocopying, mail, advertising and selling of the housing units. Both had to rely on borrowing at different stages of the development of their units of production. A particularly delicate stage in both cases was the setting up of an office. The following testimony given by Gastão illustrates the situation:

> My progress did not occur completely smoothly. There were periods of stagnation, followed by jumps, then more stagnation and another jump, and so on... In many cases, I managed to save little-by-little to meet my needs, with a little help from a loan from a friend here and there, and then I went on in stages... But the setting up of an office was the greatest jump of all... Equipment or labour you can get little-by-little, but an office, even a small one, either you have it or you do not have it... To set up an office, it has to be something good, something impressive... Because if it is shabby, I will end up losing clients, rather than gaining them. They will not even enter a shabby office... There is the rent, decoration, signs, furniture, secretary, telephone and all the rest. It has to look good... I had some money already, but I did need to borrow to supplement it... There was this chap who used to invest in my developments. He gave me some help.

102

Lastly, it was found that the only aspect of their business for which builders did not require credit was managerial capacity. As noted before, all those builders who work outside low-income settlements acquired their managerial skills through a combination of training as foremen, schooling, and/or training with their fathers. These schemes were either free, or met by the savings of the builders. Also, the expense of office staff hired to support the management structures of the builders are included within the category of overheads.

To summarize, all the builders experienced financial fluctuations in their businesses. In order to establish capitalist production they needed credit at different times for land, materials, labour, equipment and/or overheads.

The process of acquisition of credit Now, the constraints that petty-commodity builders have to acquire credit to establish capitalist production will be examined. The cases of builders who were found to lack access to credit will be presented first.

As noted before, none of the exclusive builders had access to credit, and the problems experienced by them in hiring equipment were shown in Chapter 4. Their situation regarding financial credit is similar, as described in the following statement given by Alberto:

> Sometimes I borrow money for myself, for my family. I have no choice. However, it is small quantities, just to cover an emergency. Cr$500.00, maybe Cr$1,000.00, no more than that... I cannot borrow larger quantities, to buy equipment, or whatever... When I borrow, I do so from someone I know well, who knows me well... My friends and acquaintances do not have the income to enable them to lend larger quantities, only a loan shark and of course a bank can do that... The loan sharks live on lent money, it is true, but they do not lend to everyone. They want proof that they will get the money back, plus their profit... I cannot give the proof that these sharks want. I do not even have a bank account, to give a cheque as a guarantee. I cannot give them any guarantee in terms of income, because, as you know, my situation is very unstable. And there is no point in lying, because the sharks are very well informed. They have informants all over the place. When I approach them, they already know everything about me. Where I live, what I do, everything... The other option, the bank, I cannot even think about. If I have problems in approaching a loan shark, who is much more accessible, imagine a bank, with my ragged clothes and all the rest.

The cases of the other exclusive builders replicate those of Alberto: none of them had the credentials required to acquire the credit necessary to establish capitalist production. The process and problems of obtaining credit are also shown by the cases of builders who work outside low-income settlements.

The repair and maintenance of middle- and high-cost housing, carried out using a petty-commodity form of production, did not require credit. However, it gave builders the opportunity to obtain credit. In the words of Tomas:

Things really changed when I got involved with rich clients... Some of them are really friendly, and made it clear that if I needed anything, I could count on them... The situation is not totally clear to me now, but I certainly want to expand my work, I already told you... I am counting on my clients to lend me some money, if I do not save enough.

As already noted, the construction of complete dwellings using a capitalist form of production does require credit. Nevertheless, none of the builders were able to acquire credit when working full-time in the production of low-cost housing. As demonstrated in the preceding chapter, they could only acquire the references necessary to hire equipment after they started working in the middle- and high-income market. The same holds true for the case of other forms of credit. Findings previously presented also reveal that the builders relied on their contacts outside low-income settlements to get the financial credit necessary to allow them to hire labourers. The following testimony given by Augusto further illustrates the process of acquisition of financial credit:

I needed to borrow money from time to time, I told you. To hire labourers, to transport things to begin a construction, to pay the engineer... On several occasions I have been working only doing repairs, and sudenlly comes the opportunity to build an entire house. I did not have any money at all, because I had invested my savings in my own house and in other things for my family... I do not remember the exact amounts, because they change a lot with inflation; but for the workers and to prepare the construction, it varied from Cr$10,000,00 to Cr$20.000,00, or Cr$25,000.00, plus or minus... And the engineer, charging around 1 or 2% of the price of the construction. If it is one house with two bedrooms, costing approximately Cr$1,200.000,00 today, then it would be Cr$12,000.00, or Cr$24,000.00... I could only get access to these sums after establishing myself in the south zone [middle- and high-income neighbourhoods]... My own work was my greatest reference, and I had to show what I did in the south zone... It is not that the work that I do for the poor people is bad, I do it with the same love as when working for the rich; but the poor do not have the conditions to pay for a nice job, then the result often does not look too good. I cannot go to a guy and say: 'I am a good builder, look what I have done in the shanty towns. Now lend me some money... But in the south zone, some of my clients lent me money; or I got to know other people that lent money, and I could give them the name of rich clients as references. The situation changed completely when I did that.

As shown before, the only builder who did not require financial credit throughout his career was Rafael. However, he did use hired equipment. All the remaining builders who built using a capitalist form of production needed financial credit at different moments in their careers, and for different purposes. Their experience replicate that of Augusto in terms of the process of acquisition of financial credit.

The case of the advanced capitalist builders is more complex than that of the hybrid, semi-capitalist, and capitalist builders. As shown before, they used other forms of credit besides the hire of equipment and the borrowing of money. They conducted exchange deals with landowners and building materials suppliers as well as operating condominium systems. In the words of Gustavo:

> If I could not hire tools or borrow money when I was working for the poor, you can imagine what happens with land or building materials... It is not easy to convince a landowner to exchange his plot for a flat that is still to be constructed. I have to convince him on the basis of what I have already done before... I have to show many of my previous constructions, and give him the names of many clients, who are very happy... With the materials suppliers is the same. They want to know who I am in professional terms, what guarantee they will have to get a flat built with the materials that I am asking for... The system of condominium is also a tricky business. Many people get very suspicious... If you just show them the design of a building, you have to convince them that you are able to build the whole thing... The fact that they pay less in a system of condominium helps to convince, but you still have to show them that you have a nice office, that you built nice things before, and that there have not been any problems.

In summary, the findings show that none of the builders were able to acquire the credit necessary to set up capitalist production while working in low-income settlements on a full-time basis. Next, the effects of the eventual acquisition of credity will be explained.

The effects of improving the supply of credit As in the case of the other factors examined in the previous and present chapters, the effect of the provision of credit will be analyzed through the use of policy-like situations and scenarios.

Semi-capitalist and hybrid builders have partially moved from petty-commodity to capitalist production, and the capitalist and advanced capitalist builders have moved totally. This movement was initially hindered due to lack of access to credit. However, with references acquired after entering the middle- and high-income markets, these builders gained the ability to borrow money, hire equipment, set up condominium systems and/or make exchange deals with landowners and/or building materials merchants. Therefore, access to credit enabled these builders to establish capitalist production.

However, as noted in the current and in the preceding chapters, the process of the capitalization of builders implied the loss of factors which had enabled them to produce low-cost housing previously. Testimonies already presented reveal the gradual movement of the builders away from low-cost housing production. They now have the necessary credit to acquire specialized equipment, hire skilled labourers, cover their overheads, and, in the case of advanced capitalist builders, acquire land and building materials as well. However, the use of credit leads to greater investment and therefore a larger scale of production in order to recover it. As also demonstrated, this is inconsistent with the characteristics of the demand for low-cost housing as it causes builders to lose the flexibility and structure of costs which cater for this demand. The following statement given by José adds to this argument:

Having borrowed some money, with the money then in my hands, it then becomes a big responsibility... I will invest it, but I have to pay it back, and, if it comes from a loan shark, pay back more than I borrowed... Such quantities of money do not have meaning in low-income neighbourhoods. I do not need to use them there... When I borrow money, it is to hire specialist labourers, to pay the engineer... To pay the bookkeeper, sometimes the taxes... These things belong to another type of production, you see, which is no good in low-income neighbourhoods.

Credit in the form of access to the hire of equipment also plays a role in this context. As shown in the previous chapter, builders are known to acquire many specialized equipment by hiring them. This is fundamental to their process of growth, and consequently, their abandonment of low-cost housing production. The other forms of credit encountered in the case-studies (exchange deals with landowners and materials merchants and condominium systems) are used only in speculative building. As shown before, builders only work in low-income settlements through contract building. Thus, their access to credit to commence speculative building pushes them away from low-income settlements.

In short, the cases of builders who moved away from the production of low-cost housing show the possible effect of a policy of provision of credit.

The scenarios related to the plans of the builders who produce low-cost housing will now be presented. Those builders who welcomed the possibility of the provision of credit are Juvenal, Evandro, Ronan, Augusto, Baltazar and Rafael.

As noted before, Juvenal and Augusto were planning to establish specialized units of production, and Evandro and Ronan to engage in a variety of activities ranging from repair and maintenance to the construction of complete buildings in the middle- and high-income markets. It was shown in the previous chapter that these builders welcomed a policy of provision of credit in the form of equipment for hire, and at the same time were willing to accept financial credit to purchase equipment and hire labourers. They were also willing to use financial credit in order to set up an office, and to comply with the bureaucratic procedures necessary to regularize their businesses. However, they all insisted on the need for flexible repayments, in order to counteract the fluctuations in their income. This view came from their experiences of borrowing when working outside low-income settlements. As already demonstrated, these builders rely on loans from their middle- and high-income clients, and/or from contacts established through these clients. According to the builders, although they occasionally borrow from a loan shark, they prefer to borrow from clients and contacts, because they lend for charitable rather than for profitable reasons. Although they do want the money back, they are not usually very strict in terms of the deadline for repayments. Thus, builders already use a system of flexible repayments in this regard. In the words of the hybrid builder Augusto:

My opportunity to borrow depends very much on the specific case... On how much I need, whether my acquaintances who have a good income are able to lend to me at that specific moment, even whether they are in town or not because they travel a lot... If I am really desperate, then I have to go to a loan

106

shark, but I prefer not to do so... To borrow from someone who I know personally is much, much better. It is not a business, you see, it is friendship... I explain my situation, and we make a deal... The best thing with these guys is that there is no pressure to pay back. I always try to pay as quickly as I can, in order not to have problems, and to show that I am reliable. But sometimes there are problems, delays on the payments of another contract, for instance... But these guys who lend to me know me, and they know that if I am not paying on time is not because I am cheating or something. It is because I am really in need... They are considerate, and allow me to pay bit-by-bit... When the right moment to set up my business properly comes, when there are enough good clients, I will need more money, for sure. If there is a scheme for borrowing money from the government, that would be a great help. It is a source that I would know to be there, I would not have to spend time searching around. I would go straight to the point, and the whole thing could happen quickly... But it would have to be the way we discussed, with scope for delays in the repayments.

The last part of the above testimony unveils why a policy of financial credit would benefit a builder who had already borrowed from acquaintances. It would speed up the process. Although exclusive builders never borrowed in order to invest in their businesses, they were found to be aware of the way other builders borrowed, and were keen on emulating this process. In the words of Evandro:

I know a few builders who rely on money from other people to run their businesses. But, as they told me, they borrow from people they are close to... If they have problems, they go and ask the lenders to be considerate, and wait a bit longer... This is the ideal way, in my opinion. If I can pay everything in one go, then I pay, and I even prefer to do so, in order to get rid of the loan as soon as possible... But if I cannot, I pay in instalments, sometimes of different amounts, depending on the situation.

The hybrid builder Rafael needed credit to acquire land, materials, equipment and labour, and to meet his overheads in order to establish himself in speculative construction. In contrast, the preceding builders required less sums of money, because they were planning to engage in contract building activities. Their major item of expenditure in the foreseeable future was to be the regularization of their businesses. However, their other expenses could be met in stages as the business grew. Rafael, in turn, needed a much greater amount of capital. He earned about Cr$22,000.00 per month, and, out of that, was able to save around Cr$6,000.00. His plan was to build single houses for middle-income people, but when confronted with the price of doing so, he realised that, *ceteris paribus*, he would need to save for approximately 27 years to be able to build speculatively. The average price of the construction of one square meter of a single storey medium-cost house with three bedrooms is Cr$18,764.03. Thus, a house measuring 80 square meters would cost Cr$1,501,120.00, plus Cr$450,000.00 for the land, making a total of Cr$1,951,120.00, excluding overheads. Although acknowledging the need for substantial support in terms of credit, Rafael remained very sceptical regarding the repayment of the loan, due to the uncertainties of the construction business, and he reiterated the need for flexible repayments. He already had other systems of credit in mind to alleviate the need for borrowing: hiring of equipment, and exchange deals with landowners.

In short, the scenarios presented so far show that, if appropriate credit facilities were implemented, Juvenal, Evandro, Ronan and Rafael would abandon the production of low-cost housing.

Baltazar was not willing to change his present business, but, as shown in the preceding chapter, accepted the idea of a loan to buy the equipment that he now hires. However, as in the case of the aforementioned builders, he wanted a scheme of flexible repayments to form part of any policy. The remaining builders currently producing low-cost housing were not interested in credit. As already shown, Alberto, Amin and Waldemar were planning to engage in wage-work; and João Pedro, Dorcelino and Tomas want to carry on their current work. None of these builders changed their intentions when the possibilities of obtaining credit were discussed with them.

The above cases conclude the findings about the connection between access to credit and the production of low-cost housing by petty-commodity builders. The policy-like situations of those builders currently engaged in capitalist production and the scenarios constructed through a discussion with those builders who accepted the provision of credit show that any further credit would be used to acquire the elements necessary to production which cannot be obtained through the investment from internal accumulation. The overall effect of a policy of provision of credit would be a decrease of the participation of the builders in the supply of low-cost housing.

Conclusion

This chapter began by posing a particular question, derived from one of the two general questions posed by the book. This particular question is related to growth constraints of petty-commodity producers: restrictions on access to managerial capacity and credit. Two sets of findings were presented to address these two questions.

The findings demonstrate that: (i) petty-commodity builders use a paternal system of management in low-cost housing production, and the credit required to carry out this work is negligible, (ii) capitalist production requires credit to obtain those inputs which cannot be acquired through a process of internal accumulation, and requires a managerial capacity which includes a directing authority over the labour force, its organization in a specific manner according to the production process, as well as the planning and control of the insertion of equipment and raw materials in the production process at a more complex scale than in petty-commodity production, (iii) petty-commodity builders lack access to the managerial capacity and credit required to establish capitalist production, and (iv) the provision of the managerial capacity and credit required for capitalist production leads petty-commodity builders away from low-cost housing production.

The findings corroborate the associations presented in Tables 5.1 and 5.2 (forms of production, labour processes and products which are necessary to the process of transformation of units of production). However, the findings also challenge some elements of this framework (but do not revoke them). This reiterates points noted in the conclusion of the previous chapter: (i) low-cost housing is not the only niche in petty-commodity production (and the other niche, repair and maintenance of middle- and high-cost housing, is used by the builders to escape from the low-income market), and (ii) not all the builders were willing to develop - this means that the removal of the growth constraints will lead only the petty-commodity producers who are willing to grow to move towards capitalist production, and away from low-cost housing production.

Considering the above analysis, the framework presented in Tables 5.1 and 5.2 is adjusted. The new framework is presented in Table 5.3.

Table 5.3
Revised model of Tables 5.1 and 5.2: the continuum of production including form of production, labour process, product, managerial capacity and credit

labour	PCP	Handicraft
process	CP	Elementary manufacture
	ACP	Advanced manufacture to machinofacture
product	PCP	Low-cost housing and repair of higher cost buildings
	CP and ACP	Construction of complete higher cost buildings
managerial	PCP	Paternal (for low-cost housing) and paternal
capacity		skills plus basic accountancy (for other buildings)
	CP and ACP	Increasing skills to meet the increasing complexity of production
credit	PCP	Negligible
	CP and ACP	To counteract phases of lack of internal accumulation

Key:

PCP - petty-commodity production
CP   - capitalist production
ACP - advanced capitalist production

This chapter has presented the last constraints for the capitalization of the petty-commodity builders to be analyzed in this book. Next, the main points of each chapter will be resumed and connected.

6 Conclusion

This book set out to investigate factors which enable small-scale builders to produce low-cost housing. The dynamics of change of these builders and the effect of exogenous support in their activities were central objects of analysis. An examination of the literature on the subject, presented in Chapter 1, has shown that the above-mentioned issues hitherto have not been thoroughly explained. The same holds true for the impact of the provision of support to the builders on their supply of low-cost housing.

The book has adopted a theoretical framework which conceptualizes the small-scale builders as non-capitalist producers, and uses the petty-commodity production approach to analyze them (presented in Chapter 2). It explains the differences between non-capitalist and capitalist forms of production, and the changes which occur when a given builder moves from one form to another. The framework generates two tentative answers to address the main questions posed by the book.

The first one regards the factors which enable the small-scale builders to produce low-cost housing. It suggests that these builders have a degree of flexibility and prices of services which enable them to meet the specific characteristics of the demand for low-cost housing in developing countries. For the purpose of this book, this demand is defined as being diversified, discontinuous, small-scale and capable of only erratic disbursements. The second answer suggests that if the builders are supported, they will move towards capitalist production, and lose the capacity of building low-cost housing.

The first question of the book was analyzed in Chapter 3. This question was expanded, and generated a derivative question, on the reasons why builders are capable of providing services with a degree of flexibility and price necessary to address the characteristics of the demand. The tentative answer to this question has two parts. The first explains how builders meet the demand: through the provision of services with a degree of flexibility necessary to deliver small volumes of a diversified and discontinuous output and at prices which meet the erratic disbursements of low-income people. The second part suggests that multiple skills, simple and general-purpose equipment, low costs and lack of profits enable builders to provide the aforementioned services. The findings presented in Chapter 3 confirmed both parts of this answer. Consecutively, they confirmed the correspondence between changes in the output produced by the builders - from low-cost housing to other construction activities - and the changes in the forms of production and labour processes - from petty-commodity to capitalist production, and from handicraft to manufacture and machinofacture.

These correspondences were presented in the model shown in Chapter 2 (Table 2.2). A comparative analysis of the different cases shows that the distinction between the characteristics of the builders who produce low-cost housing and those who do not, is not abrupt. There is a gradual process of change. Nevertheless, the more a builder moves along the continuum towards capitalist production, the less capacity he has to produce low-cost housing.

The empirical data also revealed limitations of the aforementioned model. The existence of repair and maintenance of middle- and high-cost housing reveals that low-cost housing is not the only activity carried out through a petty-commodity form of production in the building industry. This unveils a circumstance not envisaged in the original model. Although not invalidating it, the data shows that the model presents one possible situation, which is not universal. It relates to the correspondence between outputs, on the one side, and forms of production and labour processes, on the other. The repair and maintenance of middle- and high-cost housing actually forms an intermediate step between low-cost housing production and capitalist production. Therefore, the conceptual model of the continuum of production should include it.

The findings revealed that there are four main strategic positions in the continuum of production. First, construction of low-cost housing through petty-commodity production. Second, repair and maintenance of middle- and high-cost housing through petty-commodity production. Third, construction of complete housing and other types of buildings through capitalist production. Fourth, construction of complete housing and other types of buildings through advanced capitalist production.

The results of the study show that four of the groups of builders studied occupy a single specific position in the continuum of production: the exclusive builders are in the first position; the transitional builder is in the second; the capitalist builders are in the third; and the advanced capitalist builders in the fourth.

Conversely, three of the groups studied alternate between different positions: the mixed builders oscillate between the first and the second positions; the hybrid builders between the first, second and third; and the semi-capitalist builder between the second and third. These cases confirm that the shift from one position to another is not instantaneous. This point is further reinforced by the cases of the capitalist and advanced capitalist builders, who, in order to reach their current positions, went through transitional periods between stages. Nevertheless, a comparison of the different groups of builders highlights that a movement from petty-commodity to capitalist production is accompanied by an increasing loss of the capacity to produce low-cost housing.

The exclusive builders (the first group) had the full capacity to produce low-cost housing. The mixed builders, in turn, lose this capacity temporarily. When they had demand for repair and maintenance of middle- and high-cost housing, they extracted higher revenues than in low-cost housing production. This shows that, even within the realm of petty-commodity production, there are variations in the costs of the services of the builders. This fact influences their capacity to produce low-cost housing. However, this group is still constituted by artisanal, petty-commodity builders. They do not lose their flexibility, and are able to go back to low-income settlements quickly when it is appropriate for them. The nature of their production process makes them sufficiently agile to be able to fit in some activities in low-income settlements in parallel to activities in middle- and high-income neighbourhoods.

The transitional builder worked only in repair and maintenance of middle- and high-cost housing. Thus, his production of low-cost housing was nil. However, he still had a process of production which enabled him to go back quickly to low-income settlements, if necessary.

The hybrid builders had a larger range of activities, from low-cost housing, to the capitalist production of complete residences. They still worked in low-income settlements, when there was no demand for other activities. However, during the period in which they built complete residences, they lost the capacity of producing low-cost housing. Unlike the activities of repair and maintenance of middle- and high-cost housing, the construction of complete residences entailed a shift in the labour process, from handicraft to manufacture. However, manufacture does not have the characteristics necessary to meet the demand in low-income settlements. When the hybrid builders did not have demand for complete residences, they shifted back to petty-commodity production, but sought activities of repair and maintenance of middle- and high-cost housing. The production of low-cost housing came as a last resort.

The semi-capitalist builder also had the ability to establish capitalist production in order to construct complete residences. Like hybrid builders, there was a shift back to petty-commodity production when demand for this type of activity dwindled. Thus, although he used a labour process during some periods which enabled him to produce low-cost housing, there was sufficient demand for the repair and maintenance of middle- and high-cost housing.

The capitalist builders, producing complete buildings on a full-time basis, lost the capacity to produce low-cost housing completely. The advanced capitalist builders, in turn, are even more distant from low-cost housing production, because their specialized equipment and skills, higher structure of costs and profits entail higher rigidity and higher prices beyond the reach of the specific type of demand encountered in low-income settlements.

The second main question of this book was examined in Chapters 4 and 5. It relates to the factors which limit the capitalization of the small-scale builders, and the effect of their provision on the production of low-cost housing. This main question generates derivative questions related to different factors: equipment, labour capacity, managerial capacity and credit.

Data regarding the activities of builders in low-income settlements show that low-cost housing production is characterized by simple and multi-purpose equipment, unskilled labour, paternal management and negligible need for credit. However, it is important to make some clarifications. Specialized equipment and semi-skilled labour are also found in low-cost housing production, although on a modest scale.

The findings also reveal that the exclusive builders did not have the necessary savings to pay assistants to produce low-cost housing. This fact could suggest that there is a need for credit. However, even without credit, these builders managed to produce low-cost housing - either enroling in activities which do not demand assistants, and/or securing advanced payment from the clients.

Data regarding the builders who use a capitalist form of production show that capitalist production requires: (i) specialized equipment, (ii) labour capacity able to accomplish the specific tasks to be carried out in each stage of the construction process, (iii) credit to obtain the elements necessary for production which cannot be acquired through a process of internal accumulation, and (iv) managerial capacity which includes a directing authority over the labour force, its organization in a specific manner according to the production process, the planning and control of the insertion of equipment and raw materials in the production process at a more complex scale than in petty-commodity production.

The aim of the presentation of the above findings is to reveal the differences between petty-commodity production of low-cost housing and capitalist production of other types of buildings. The next set of findings show that the small-scale (petty-commodity) builders do not have access to the factors necessary to establish capitalist production. The findings also revealed that the problems faced by petty-commodity builders vary according to the niche of the market in which they operate. Builders engaged in repair and maintenance of middle- and high-cost housing do not have the same problems as those engaged only in low-cost housing production. These findings revealed the way in which the builders who managed to grow overcome their constraints: their entry into the middle- and high-income markets through petty-commodity activities enabled them to acquire savings and references which, in turn, gave them access to equipment, labour capacity, managerial capacity and the credit required for capitalist production. The fact that a number of builders grew through this way, without supporting policies, does not imply that it is useless to study the possible effect of the provision of the above mentioned factors. Actually, as already shown, the findings include the case of builders who are willing to capitalize, but are constrained by the lack of one or more factors.

The last set of findings show that the provision of equipment, labour capacity, managerial capacity and credit required for capitalist production will lead the small-scale (petty-commodity) builders away from low-cost housing production. The builders who work in low-income settlements and who want to establish or expand capitalist production are planning to obtain the necessary factors through the process already described - i.e. increasing activity in the middle- and high-income markets, first, through petty-commodity activities, in order to acquire the necessary savings and references. These plans are based on the builders' supposition that there is no alternative available - e.g. there is no supporting policy. Considering this situation, the implementation of a policy of provision of equipment, labour capacity, managerial capacity and credit could affect a given builder in two ways. First, assuming that he would not be able to acquire these factors on his own, then the policy would actually *open up* the possibility of capitalization for him. Second, assuming that the builder would be successful on his own, then the policy would *speed up* his development. In both cases, the outcome is a move in the continuum of production towards capitalization, and away from the construction of low-cost housing.

The analysis carried out in previous chapters already has unveiled connections between different sets of findings. The major combined conclusion of all the findings regards the existence of a relationship between the provision of equipment, labour capacity, managerial capacity and credit; the movement of the builders along the continuum from non-capitalist (petty-commodity) to capitalist production; the loss of the characteristics which enable them to produce low-cost housing; and their consequent discontinuation of low-cost housing production. This statement is the major conclusion of this book.

The analysis of the different factors also has shown that, even if the builder is willing to develop, the provision of each factor alone is not enough for supporting him, for the other factors are also important. For instance, it has been shown that in low-cost housing production there is a strong personal contact between the builders and their labourers. When the scale of their workforce increases, this contact weakens. However, if the personal contact is not replaced by a proper directing management, the whole production collapses. This finding reveals that, even when labour capacity is provided to the builders, they still need the managerial capacity to handle it. By the same token, there is no point in having access to skilled labourers, if the builders do not have the specialized equipment to establish capitalist production. Still, even having access to equipment and managerial and labour capacity, the builders need credit to acquire further elements necessary for capitalist production.

Even the provision of the four factors analyzed may not guarantee the development of the builders who have motivation and self-confidence to invest in their units of production. Other factors also have been theorized in Chapter 2. Although some of these factors have been approached through the provision of credit, like building materials, others are not placed in this context (e.g. building standards and regulations). However, rather than attempting to cover all the possible factors which influence the process of capitalization of the builders, this book opted to concentrate on four of them.

Theoretical framework

The way the empirical findings support the theory previously developed reveals that: the petty-commodity production approach to small-scale low-cost housing provision in developing countries is a useful tool to construct a theoretical framework to address the specific questions of this book.

However, this theoretical approach also has its limitations, which have been analyzed in Chapter 1. Thus, its use here does not automatically support the approach as a valuable basis to answer other questions related to the field of inquiry in which this book is placed, let alone other fields.

This book has connected the petty-commodity form of production with an artisanal labour process, a capitalist form with an elementary manufacturing process, and an advanced capitalist form with advanced manufacture and machinofacture. As shown in Chapter 2, the book also acknowledges that the above associations do not cover the whole universe of possibilities. A given labour process may be related to other forms and modes of production - e.g. handicraft with feudalism. Moreover, the empirical findings have shown that capitalization is not the only possible transformation to occur in petty-commodity production, as, for instance, some totally independent contract builders may move towards wage-labour. Such possibilities have also been recognized in theoretical terms in Chapter 2. However, as noted in that chapter, the aim of this book is to study specifically factors related to the passage from the particular stage of handicraft petty-commodity production to manufacture capitalist production, from there to manufacture advanced capitalism, and then to mixed manufacture/ machinofacture advanced capitalism.

A basic model of the continuum of production, constructed without the information of the empirical evidence, is presented in Table 6.1. Based on the research findings, this model is modified, as shown in Table 6.2.

Table 6.1
The continuum of production including form of production, labour process, product, equipment, labour capacity, managerial capacity and credit

labour	PCP	Handicraft
process	CP	Elementary manufacture
	ACP	Advanced manufacture to machinofacture
product	PCP	Low-cost housing
	CP and ACP	Other types of buildings
equipment	PCP	Simple, general purpose
	CP and ACP	Specialized equipment
labour	PCP	Unskilled labour
capacity	CP	Increasing predominance of skilled labour
	ACP	Decrease in skills
managerial	PCP	Paternal
capacity	CP and ACP	Increasing skills to meet the increasing complexity of production
credit	PCP	Negligible
	CP and ACP	To counteract phases of lack of internal accumulation

Key:

PCP - petty-commodity production
CP - capitalist production
ACP - advanced capitalist production

Table 6.2
Revised model of Table 6.1

labour	PCP	Handicraft
process	CP	Elementary manufacture
	ACP	Advanced manufacture to machinofacture
product	PCP	Low-cost housing and repair of higher cost buildings
	CP and ACP	Construction of complete higher cost buildings
equipment	PCP	Simple general purpose (for low-cost housing) and same set plus (mainly small-scale) specialized equipment (for other buildings)
	CP and ACP	Increasing predominance of specialized equipment
labour	PCP	Predominance of unskilled labour
capacity	CP	Increasing predominance of skilled labour
	ACP	Decrease in skills
managerial	PCP	Paternal (for low-cost housing) and paternal skills plus basic accountancy (for other buildings)
capacity	CP and ACP	Increasing skills to meet the increasing complexity of production
credit	PCP	Negligible
	CP and ACP	To counteract phases of lack of internal accumulation

Key:

PCP - petty-commodity production
CP - capitalist production
ACP - advanced capitalist production

Having shown the connection between the findings and the theoretical framework, the policy implications of the research will now be discussed.

Policies

Regarding specific policies of support for builders, the book has unveiled the importance of provision of equipment, flexible repayments for financial credit, and managerial training.

Equipment for hire plays an important role in the process of development of the small-scale builders, and it is therefore suggested that it should be fostered. Based on the experience of the builders interviewed, the expansion of the hire scheme is not sufficient. A major problem that needs to be tackled is the obliteration of the bureaucracy in order to facilitate the hiring process. The implementation of ways to foster the supply of equipment for sale would also be advantageous, especially those which include cost reduction. The findings show that recuperation of scrap equipment and the access to second hand tools is very dispersed. Thus, it is important to support the establishment of venues for the sale of second-hand equipment, which would facilitate access to suppliers and buyers, who would benefit from economies of agglomeration. It could be accompanied by an increase in the recuperation of scrap. However, considering the extreme fluctuations that the small-scale builders have faced in terms of income generation and capacity to save, proposals related to equipment for sale could be implemented in parallel to those related to hiring - but should not replace them. As shown, a number of builders have faced income difficulties to buy even second-hand equipment. Thus, equipment for hire is fundamental to cushion the builders in hard times - as also demonstrated, even capitalist builders still hire equipment.

Financial credit is important as a way to provide access to the different factors necessary to establish capitalist production. All the builders who are willing to accept credit have shown concern with problems that they could have to meet fixed repayments. They suggested the possibility of flexible repayments, based on informal ways of borrowing, which prevail between the builders and their friends and acquaintances. Therefore, it would be helpful to devise financing schemes specifically appropriate to their particular conditions.

As for the training of the workforce, the problem is less grave, at least in the specific country where primary data for this book was collected. The on-the-job scheme which is currently under way on the building industry in Brazil suits the needs of the builders in their process of development. Expansion of the training scheme would be advantageous, but the major problem for the builders concerns the gathering of a reserve fund to hire the labourers. This issue leads to provision of credit, already stressed. The alternative of diminishing the need for skilled labourers through the use of capital intensive technology encountered a number of problems. Firstly, the construction industry in Brazil (as well as throughout the developing world) is not fully mechanized. Secondly, mechanization itself requires an initial investment, which is a major problem for the builders. Thirdly, the exclusive builders do not have the necessary skills to assess the economies of capital-intensive technology accurately.

The situation in terms of managerial training is different. The small-scale builders who capitalized relied on different combinations of four schemes: family training, training as foreman, elementary schooling, and on-the-job training in repair and maintenance of middle- and high-cost housing. However, such conditions are not open for all. Therefore, the setting up of managerial training schemes is also important. The price of the existing training schemes is not really a problem. The problem, according to the builders, is the loss of work time to attend a course. Although this could be beneficial in the long-run, it is not feasible because they live on a subsistence level, and need to maximize their working time. A further problem of the existing training schemes is that they are not in close proximity to the neighbourhoods where the builders live. The builders need to be present as much as possible in their neighbourhoods to capture work, as the market is extremely volatile and requires small-scale services. Based on this situation and on the demands of the builders themselves, a solution would be a training scheme with a maintenance grant, or the establishment of decentralized/mobile training centres in the builders' neighbourhoods, with courses extending over a longer period to accommodate only a few hours of study per week.

The relation between the provision of given factors and the capitalization of the small-scale builders does not mean that small-scale low-cost housing production will disappear, for the lacunae left empty by the builders which move will be filled by newcomers. However, the findings of the book suggest that, other things being equal, *support for these builders will not increase their participation in the production of low-cost housing*. The findings from a number of case-studies cannot be used to affirm categorically that the same result will be found in the case of a massive support for small-scale builders on a large-scale. Under such conditions, other factors which do not appear in the cases studied may be present, thus altering the situation. Nevertheless, the findings do reveal the existence of a tendency. They also reveal that, due to the current income situation of the lower strata of the population, low-cost housing nowadays is the *last resort* for the builders. The revenue which a builder extracts in low-cost housing production is lower than that of other building activities, and the builders would leave low-cost housing production as soon as another opportunity arises.

This reasoning could lead to the conclusion that the aforementioned policies entail a waste of resources in respect to the amelioration of the housing situation of the low-income population (because such policies would diminish the participation of the small-scale builders in the production of low-cost housing). However, rather than not supporting the builders and/or preventing them from capitalizing, more effective actions can be taken.

One way of attracting the builders to low-cost housing production is to implement policies for fostering the demand. There is a debate regarding small-scale production in general and the specific issue of demand, which is worth mentioning here.

Piore and Sabel, for instance, suggest that the fordist system of large-scale production needs institutional mechanisms of macroeconomic regulations in order to create, maintain or expand demand, for it needs large-scale demand. These authors argue that post-fordist processes, which they term flexible specialization, based on small-scale units, do not need regulation. This happens because the units have the flexibility to adapt to different patterns of demand and enter different niches in the market (Piore and Sabel, 1984). However, Schmitz responds that in our view this is a flaw. It would only be correct as long as flexible specialisation accounts for a small part of industrial activity. The more generalised flexible specialisation becomes the more the level of aggregate demand matters for its sustainability. Hence, institutional mechanisms to maintain or raise this demand are far from superfluous... The question of demand management arises irrespective of whether goods are mass produced or made in small batches. Separating flexible specialisation from issues of macroeconomic demand implies that flexible specialisation is an exception, that it can only fill the cracks, that it remains limited to exploiting tiny niches in the market (Schmitz, 1989, pp. 36-37).

This book takes the second position, and, connecting it to the field of housing production, suggests that small-scale builders, either pre-fordist (e.g. petty-commodity producers) or post-fordist, need regulation of demand in order to expand their activities in low-income settlements, or else they would not have incentives to cater for an insecure and low-revenue yielding sector of the market.

On the supply side, a question to be asked is how can builders be supported, and, at the same time, to ensure that their participation on low-cost housing production increases. The support given to small-scale builders may, anyway, fortify the building industry as whole, as it entails improvements in equipment, credit, managerial and labour force capacity, and the like. However, considering that the support bolsters the current structure of capitalist production within the industry - by the opening up of possibilities for capitalization of petty-commodity builders - it will not ameliorate automatically the provision of low-cost housing. One rather obvious alternative would be to foster the participation of the existent types of capitalist units of production in the low-income market. However, considering that such units do not have the attributes to satisfy the characteristics of the current demand, this alternative would have to be accompanied by a policy of altering the structure of production of the units and/or the demand.

A more consistent alternative on the supply side would be to implement policies of supporting the development of the builders along post-fordist tendencies examined in Chapter 2 (i.e. towards small-scale but technologically sophisticated flexible units of production, rather than towards the current large-scale mass production-oriented ones). The idea is that there are similarities between the petty-commodity process used by the small-scale builders and the post-fordist tendencies in the building industry (e.g. Werna, 1994). As Ball puts it,

the pendulum [now] has swung in favour of smaller concerns with lower overheads and great management flexibility (Ball, 1988b, p. 185).

This shows that the post-fordist trends contain characteristics of petty-commodity production, emphasised previously (Chapters 2 and 3). This issue is supported by Piore and Sabel, who point out the existence of two paths of technological development throughout the different branches of industry: crafts and mass production. The latter path has prevailed over the former until the 1970s, but the new, flexible specialization tendencies originate from the former path (Piore and Sabel, 1984). In short, flexible specialization does not represent something totally new, but rather the resumption and development of an already existent path of technological development which has been overshadowed by mass production. Through the development of the aforementioned scheme, the builders could still meet a demand which is discontinuous, diverse, small-scale and with erratic disbursements. However, they would tackle it with a higher productivity, which would increase their revenues, thus giving them more incentives to produce low-cost housing. This upgrading could also enable the builders to set up a few, rather than one, small-scale production teams, thus further increasing their revenue possibilities.

Therefore, management training, provision of equipment and credit facilities should be oriented in this direction. In terms of workforce training, the current on-the-job scheme would still suit the needs of the development along the trend above mentioned. However, depending on the level of skills required in the upgraded units of production, wage levels should be raised, to ensure that jobs in this sector would be attractive, as opposed to large-scale units of production. The possibility of setting up a number of small-scale teams rather than just one under the direction of the same builder also touches upon the question of wages. The builders interviewed who have tried this scheme have had bad experiences. If the builder works alongside his labourers, there is no problem. In an absentee situation, their tight relationship loosens, and the labourers tend to work less and/or demand higher pay, because they assume to be doing the whole work rather than just helping the master builder. Therefore, higher wages would be an important motivation for the labourers to move from working under a scheme of parental management to more independent activities.

Further research

Avenues for further research based on different issues discussed throughout this chapter include large-scale low-cost housing production, the transition from small-scale petty-commodity production to post-fordist processes, and the relation between the construction activities of the builders and other sources of income generation.

The first avenue should focus on the conditions in which large-scale capitalist units of production have been able to reach the low-income market in other parts of the world. It could reveal suggestions on how to implement the contribution of these units elsewhere.

The second avenue regards the relationship between petty-commodity production units and the post-fordist tendencies, already emphasised. This research would contribute to the understanding of petty-commodity type of production with an advanced process of production.

The third avenue encompasses the relation between the construction activities of the builders and other parallel income generating activities, such as wage-labour, the setting up of a business outside the building industry, or the supporting work of the wives. While this book has been basically concerned with the process of production of the builders and therefore does not concentrate on the aforementioned relations, it would be interesting to see how the process of development of the builders is actually supported or hampered by other activities.

Scope of the findings

The application of findings accruing from a number of cases from a given country to other instances clearly requires caution. However, the general situation encountered throughout the developing world suggests that the findings of this book have relevance which go beyond its specific context. As already shown, the participation of small-scale/petty-commodity builders in the production of low-cost housing has been verified in many other developing countries. Similarly, the characteristics of the demand which they address is not confined to Belo Horizonte or Brazil. Moreover, although the Brazilian building industry is at a more advanced stage than its counterparts in many other developing countries, the increasing penetration of capitalism all over the world has been widely documented. Thus, whether capitalism is still incipient or already advanced in a given country, it is reasonable to conclude that the support given to builders in the form of provision of factors necessary to establish capitalist production is likely to reinforce their growth. Consequently, the inferences from this book could contribute as one of the many foundations necessary to design policies which benefit both small-scale builders and those in need of shelter.

Bibliography

Aguiar Jr., F. (1989), 'The Philippine Peasant as Capitalist: Beyond the Categories of Ideal-Typical Capitalism', *Journal of Peasant Studies*, 17:1, pp. 41-67.

Almanaque Abril (1985), *Almanaque Abril*, Editora Abril, São Paulo.

Almanaque Abril (1995), *Almanaque Abril*, Editora Abril, São Paulo.

Ayatta, S. (1986), 'Economic Growth and Petty-Commodity Production in Turkey', in Scott A. (ed.), 'Rethinking Petty-Commodity Production', *Social Analysis*, Special Issue Series, 20, pp. 79-92.

Balibar, E. (1966), 'Sur les Concepts Fondamentaux du Materialisme Historique', in Althusser, L. and Balibar, E. (eds), *Lire le Capital - Tome II*, Maspero, Paris, pp. 187-332.

Ball, M. (1983), 'Housing Production: Do We Need a New Research Programme or a New Type of Housing Research?', paper presented at Social Science Research Council Conference on 'Housing in Britain; The Next Decade', London.

Ball, M. (1986), 'Housing Analysis: Time for a Theoretical Refocus?', *Housing Studies*, 1:3, pp. 147-165.

Ball, M. (1988a), *Rebuilding Construction: economic change in the British construction industry*, Routledge, London.

Ball, M. (1988b), 'The International Restructuring of Housing Production', in Ball, M; Harloe, M. and Martens, M. (eds), *Housing and Social Change in Europe and the USA*, Routledge, New York, pp. 169-198.

Basok, T. (1989), 'How Useful is the 'Petty Commodity Production' Approach? Explaining the Survival and Success of Small Salvadorean Urban Enterprises in Costa Rica', *Labour, Capital and Society*, 22:1, pp. 41-64.

Beldecos, G. (1987), 'Transformation of the Built Environment and Speculative Housebuilding in Inner Athens, 1955-1974', M.Phil. dissertation, University College London.

Bernstein, H. (1986), 'Is There a Concept of Petty-Commodity Production Generic to Capitalism?', paper presented at the Thirteen European Congress for Rural Sociology, Braga.

Bernstein, H. (1988), 'Capitalism and Petty-Bourgeois Production: Class Relations and Divisions of Labour', *Journal of Peasant Studies*, 15:2, pp. 258-271.

Bettelheim, C. (1972), 'Theoretical Comments', in Emmanuel, A. (ed.), *Unequal Exchange - A Study of the Imperialism of Trade*, New Left Books, London, pp. 271-322.

Bienefeld, M. (1979), 'The Informal Sector and Peripheral Capitalism: the Case of Tanzania', *Bulletin of the Institute of Development Studies*, 6:3, pp. 53-73.

Bienefeld, M. and Godfrey, M. (1975), 'Measuring Unemployment and the Informal Sector. Some Conceptual and Statistical Problems', *Bulletin of the Institute of Development Studies*, 7:3, pp. 4-10.

Blincow, M. (1986), 'Scavengers and Recycling: A Neglected Domain of Production', *Labour, Capital and Society*, 19:1, pp. 94-115.

Bonduki, N. and Rolnick, R. (1979), 'Periferia da Grande São Paulo: Reprodução do Espaço como Expediente da Reprodução da Força de Trabalho', in Maricato, E. (ed.), *A Produção Capitalista da Casa (e da Cidade) no Brasil Industrial*, Alfa-Omega, São Paulo, pp. 117-154.

Bonke, S. and Goth, S. (1983), 'The Labour Process in the Construction Industry', *The Production of The Built Environment - Proceedings of the 1982 Bartlett International Summer School*, Bartlett School of Architecture and Planning, London, pp. 1-2/1-9.

Bonke, S. and Jensen, P. (1982), 'Technical Development and Employment in The Danish Building Industry', *The Production of The Built Environment - Proceedings of the 3rd. Bartlett International Summer School*, Bartlett School of Architecture and Planning, London, pp. 4-4/4-9.

Brewer, A. (1984), *A Guide to Marx's Capital*, Cambridge University Press, Cambridge.

Brighton Labour Process Group (1977), 'The Capitalist Labour Process', *Capital and Class*, 1, Spring, pp. 3-26.

Bristol, G. (1991), 'Role and Responsibilities - The Future of Architecture in Housing Delivery', *Proceedings of the International Association for Housing Science World Congress - Habitat for the 21st. Century*, International Association for Housing Science (in association with Ecole des Mines D'Alés & Florida International University), Alés, pp. 720-731.

Bromley, R. (1985), 'Preface', in Bromley, R. (ed.), *Planning for Small Enterprises in Third World Cities*, Pergamon Press, Oxford, pp. v-viii.

Bruce, J. and Dwyer, D. (eds) (1988), *A Home Divided: Women and Income*, Stanford University Press, Stanford.

Burgess, R. (1978), 'Petty commodity housing or dweller control? A critique of John Turner's views on housing policy', *World Development*, 6:9/10, pp. 1105-1134.

Burgess, R. (1982), 'Self-Help Housing Advocacy: A Curious Form of Radicalism. A Critique of the Work of John F. C. Turner', in Ward, P. (ed.), *Self-Help Housing - A Critique*, Mansell, London, pp. 55-97.

Burgess, R. (1992), 'Helping Some to Help Themselves: Third World Housing Policies and Development Strategies', in Mathey, K. (ed.), *Beyond Self-Help Housing*, Mansell, London, pp. 75-91.

Busuttil, S. (1987), 'Houselessness and the training problem', *Cities*, 4:2, pp. 152-158.

Cardoso, A. and Short, J. (1983), 'Forms of Housing Production: Initial Formulations', *Environment and Planning A*, 15, pp. 917-928.

Castells, M. (1980), 'Multinational Capital, National States, and Local Communities', I.U.R.D. Working Paper, University of California, Berkeley.

Castells, M. and Portes, A. (1989), 'World Underneath: The Origins, Dynamics, and Effects of the Informal Economy', in Portes, A., Castells, M. and Benton, L. (eds), *The Informal Economy - Studies in Advanced and Less Developed Countries*, The John Hopkins University Press, Baltimore, pp. 11-37.

Chinosa, N. (1982), 'The Construction Industry and Explanations for Non-Development: Policies and Framework for the Development of Small Firms in Developing Countries', M.Sc. dissertation, University College London.

Christian, J. (1987), 'The Contribution of Shelter to National Economic Development', *Proceedings of the Second International Shelter Conference and Vienna Recommendations on Shelter and Urban Development*, National Association of Realtors, Washington, pp. 50-55.

Collier, D. (1976), *Squatters and Oligarchs*, John Hopkins University Press, Baltimore.

Cortez, J. (1979), 'Small Enterprises Development Corporation (SEDCO): An Approach to Developing the Local Construction Industry', International Labour Office, Construction and Management Programme, Management Development Branch, Training Department, GP - ILO/1067, Geneva.

Davies, R. (1979), 'Informal sector or subordinate mode of production? A model', in Bromley, R. and Gerry, C. (eds), *Casual Work and Poverty in Third World Cities*, John Wiley & Sons, Chichester, pp. 87-104.

Dickson, D. (1974), *Alternative Technology and the Politics of Technical Change*, William Collin Sons & Co., Glasgow.

Drakakis-Smith, D. (1981), *Urbanisation, Housing and the Development Process*, Croom Helm, London.

Drewer, S. (1975), 'The Construction Industry in Developing Countries - A Framework for Planning', Building Economics Research Unit, University College London, mimeo.

Durand-Lasserve, A. (1987), 'Land and Housing in Third World Cities: are public and private strategies contradictory?', *Cities*, 4:4, pp. 325-338.

Edmonds, G. and Miles, D. (1984), *Foundations for Change - Aspects of the Construction Industry in Developing Countries*, Intermediate Technology Publications, London.

Foley, D. (1986), *Understanding capital: Marx's economic theory*, Harvard University Press, Cambridge (Mass.).

Friedman, H. (1980), 'Household Production and the National Economy: Concepts for the Analysis of Agrarian Formations', *Journal of Peasant Studies*, 7:1, pp. 158-184.

Fundação João Pinheiro (1984), *Diagnóstico Nacional da Indústria da Construção - Volume 4 - O Processo Construtivo*, Fundação João Pinheiro, Belo Horizonte.

Ganesan, S. (1982), *Management of Small Construction Firms*, Asia Productivity Organisation, Tokyo.

Ganesan, S. (1983), 'Housing and Construction: Major Constraints and Development Measures', *Habitat International*, 7:5/6, pp. 173-194.

Gerry, C. (1978), 'Petty Production and Capitalist Production in Dakar: The Crisis of the Self-Employed', *World Development*, 6:9/10, pp. 1147-1160.

Gerry, C. (1979), 'Small-Scale Manufacturing and Repairs in Dakar: A Survey of Market Relations within the Urban Economy', in Bromley, R. and Gerry, C. (eds), *Casual Work and Poverty in Third World Cities*, John Wiley & Sons, Chichester, pp. 229-250.

Gerry, C. and Birkbeck, C. (1981), 'The Petty-Commodity Producer in Third World Cities: Petit Bourgeois or 'Disguised Proletarian'?', in Bechofer, F. and Elliot, B. (eds), *The Petite Bourgeoisie: Comparative Studies of an Uneasy Stratum*, Macmillan, London, pp. 121-154.

Gertler, M. (1988), 'The Limits to Flexibility: Comments on the Post-Fordist Vision of Production and its Geography', Department of Geography, University of Toronto, mimeo.

Gibson, P. and Neocosmos, M. (1985), 'Some Problems in the Political Economy of 'African Socialism'', in Bernstein, H. and Campbell, B. (eds), *Contradictions of Accumulation in Africa. Studies in Economy and State*, Sage, Beverly Hills, pp. 153-206.

Gilbert, A. (1986), 'Self-Help Housing and State Intervention: Illustrative Reflections on the Petty Commodity Production Debate', in Drakakis-Smith, D. (ed.), *Urbanisation in the Developing World*, Croom Helm, London, pp. 175-194.

Gilbert, R. (1982), 'The Limitations of the Employment Function of the Construction Sector: The Case of Brazil', Ph.D. dissertation, University College London.

Glewwe, P. and Van der Gaag, J. (1990), 'Identifying the Poor in Developing Countries: Do Different Definitions Matter?', *World Development*, 18:6, pp. 803-814.

Godelier, M. (1978), *Perspectives in Marxist Anthropology*, Cambridge University Press, Cambridge.

Goethert, R. and Hamdi, N. (1988), *Making Microplans: A community based process in programming and development*, Intermediate Technology Publications, London.

Gogh, K. (1990), 'The Colombian Building Materials Industry: Transformation or Stagnation?' paper presented at the 11th. Bartlett International Summer School, Moscow.

Goth, S. (1984), 'Construction Management and Control over the Construction Labour Process', *The Production of The Built Environment - Proceedings of the 5th. Bartlett International Summer School*, Bartlett School of Architecture and Planning, London, pp. 4-3/4-7.

Grandi, S. (1985), 'Desenvolvimento da Indústria da Construção no Brasil: Mobilidade e Acumulação do Capital e da Força de Trabalho', Ph.D. dissertation, Universidade de São Paulo.

Hamdi, N. and Goethert, R. (1989), 'The Support Paradigm for Housing and its Impacts on Practice', *Habitat International*, 13:4, pp. 19-28.

Harloe, M. (1988), 'Towards a New Politics of Housing Provision', in Ball, M; Harloe, M. and Martens, M. (eds), *Housing and Social Change in Europe and the USA*, Routledge, New York, pp. 199-217.

Harms, H. (1982), 'Historical Perspectives on the Practice and Purpose of Self-Help Housing', in Ward, P. (ed.), *Self-Help Housing - A Critique*, Mansell, London, pp. 15-55.

Hart, K. (1971), 'Informal Income Opportunities and Urban Employment in Ghana', paper presented at the Institute of Development Studies Conference on Urban Unemployment in Africa, University of Sussex; revised version published in *The Journal of Modern African Studies*, 11:1, pp. 61-89, 1973.

Harvey, D. (1989), *The Condition of Post-Modernity - an Inquiry into the Origins of Cultural Change*, Basil Blackwell, Oxford.

Henriod, E. (1984), *The Construction Industry - Issues and Strategies in Developing Countries*, The World Bank, Washington.

IBAM (Instituto Brasileiro de Administração Municipal) (1982), *Processo de Crescimento e Ocupação da Periferia*, IBAM, Rio de Janeiro.

IBAM (Instituto Brasileiro de Administração Municipal) (1986), 'Urbanização da Favela Marcílio Dias', Research Report, convênio IBAM/BNH, Rio de Janeiro.

IBGE (Instituto Brasileiro de Geografia e Estatística) (1983), *Belo Horizonte*, IBGE, Rio de Janeiro.

ILO (International Labour Office) (1972), *Employment, Incomes and Equality: A Strategy for Increasing Productive Employment in Kenya*, ILO, Geneva.

Inyang, I. (1987), 'Non-Conventional Housing in Nigeria - The Case of Calabar', M.Phil. dissertation, University of Edinburgh.

IPT (Instituto de Pesquisas Tecnológicas do Estado de São Paulo) (1988), *Programa de Atualização Tecnológica Industrial - PATI - Construção Habitacional*, Secretaria de Ciência e Tecnologia do Estado de São Paulo, São Paulo.

Isik, O. (1992), 'The Penetration of Capitalism into Housing Production - Speculative House Building in Turkey 1950-1980', Ph.D. dissertation, University College London.

IT Building (undated), 'A Management Handbook for the Nigeria Building Contractor', Information Paper n. 9, Intermediate Technology Development Group, London.

Jackson, S. (1971), 'Economically Appropriate Technologies for Developing Countries', Occasional Paper Series n. 3, Overseas Development Council, Washington.

Jequier, N. (1976), *Appropriate Technology: Problems and Promises*, Development Centre Studies, OECD, Paris.

Jessop, B. (1990), 'Fordism and Postfordism: a critical reformulation', paper presented at the Conference on Pathways to Industrialization and Regional Development, Lake Arrowhead.

Johnstone, M. (1978), 'Unconventional Housing in West Malaysian Cities: A Preliminary Inquiry', in Rimmer, P.; Drakakis-Smith, D. and McGee T. (eds), *Food, Shelter and Transportation in the Southeast Asia and the Pacific*, Research School of Pacific Studies, Department of Human Geography, Publication HG/12, The Australian National University, Canberra, pp. 111-129.

Johnstone, M. (1984), 'Urban Housing and Housing Policy in Peninsular Malaysia', *International Journal of Urban and Regional Research*, 8:4, pp. 497-529.

Kaplinsky, R. (1985), 'Electronics based automation technology and the onset of systemofacture: implications for Third World development', *World Development*, 13:3, pp. 423-440.

Kaplinsky, R. (1990), 'The Economies of Small - Appropriate technology in a changing world', Intermediate Technology Publications, London.

Kitay, M. (1987), 'Public-Private Sector Co-operation for the Development of Low-Income Shelter', *Habitat International*, 11:1, pp. 29-36.

Kowarick, L. (1979), 'Capitalism and Urban Marginality in Brazil', in Bromley, R. and Gerry, C. (eds), *Casual Work and Poverty in Third World Cities*, John Wiley & Sons, Chichester, pp. 69-85.

Laclau, E. (1971), 'Feudalism and Capitalism in Latin America', *New Left Review*, 67, pp. 19-38.

Lanzetta, M. and Murillo, G. (1989), 'The Articulation of Formal and Informal Sectors in the Economy of Bogota, Colombia', in Portes, A., Castells, M. and Benton, L. (eds), *The Informal Economy - Studies in Advanced and Less Developed Countries*, The John Hopkins University Press, Baltimore, pp. 95-110.

Le Brun, O. and Gerry, C. (1975), 'Petty Producers and Capitalism', *Review of African Political Economy*, 3, pp. 20-32.

Levin, R. and Neocosmos, M. (1989), 'The Agrarian Question and Class Contradictions in South Africa: Some Theoretical Considerations', *Journal of Peasant Studies*, 16:2, pp. 230-259.

Leys, C. (1975), *Underdevelopment in Kenya - The Political Economy of Neo-Colonialism*, Heinemann, London.

Liberaki, A. (1988), 'Small Firms and Flexible Specialization in the Greek Industry', Ph.D. dissertation, University of Sussex.

Lintz, R. (1989), 'Support Strategies for Informal Production of Housing and Urban Services', Office of Housing and Urban Programs, United States Agency for International Development.

Lipsey, R. (1971), *Introduction to Positive Economics*, Third Edition, Weidenfeld & Nicolson, London.

Long, N. and Richardson, P. (1978), 'Informal Sector, Petty-Commodity Production and the Social Relations of Small Scale Enterprise', in Clammer, J. (ed.), *The New Economic Anthropology*, Macmillan, London, pp. 176-200.

Lovering, J. (1991), 'Theorizing postfordism: why contingency matters (a further response to Scott)', *International Journal of Urban and Regional Research*, 15:2, pp. 298-301.

Maricato, E. (1987), *Política Habitacional no Regime Militar - Do Milagre Brasileiro à Crise Econômica*, Vozes, Petrópolis.

Marx, K. (1977), *Capital* (three volumes), Lawrence and Wishart, London.

Mautner, Y. (1987), 'The building industry which works at the fringes of capitalism: the case of São Paulo', *The Production of The Built Environment - Proceedings of the 8th Bartlett International Summer School*, Bartlett School of Architecture and Planning, London, pp. 168-175.

Mautner, Y. (1989), 'The periphery as a frontier for the expansion of capital', *The Production of the Built Environment - Proceedings of the 10th. Bartlett*

International Summer School, Bartlett School of Architecture and Planning, London, pp. 132-138.

Mautner, Y. (1991), 'The Periphery as a Frontier for the Expansion of Capital', Ph.D. dissertation, University College London.

Mayo, S.; Malpezzi, S. and Cross, D. (1986), 'Shelter Strategies for the Urban Poor in Developing Countries', *World Bank Research Observer*, 2, pp. 183-204.

Mazundar, D. (1975), 'The Urban Informal Sector', World Bank Staff Working Paper n. 211, Washington.

Meillassoux, C. (1980), 'From reproduction to production: a Marxist approach to economic anthropology', in Wolpe, H. (ed.) (1980), *The Articulation of Modes of Production*, Routledge & Kegan Paul, London, pp. 189-201.

Miles, D. and Parker, M. (1984), 'Housing for the Poor', *Appropriate Technology*, 11:3, pp. 1-4.

Moavenzadeh, F. (1987), 'The Construction Industry', in Rodwin, L. (ed.), *Shelter, Settlement and Development*, Allen & Unwin, Boston, pp. 73-107.

Moser, C. (1982), 'A home of one's own: squatter housing strategies in Guayaquil, Ecuador', in Gilbert, A. with Hardoy, J. and Ramirez, R. (eds), *Urbanization in Contemporary Latin America: Critical Approaches to the Analysis of Urban Issues*, John Wiley & Sons, Chichester, pp. 159-190.

Moser, C. (1984), 'The Informal Sector Reworked: Viability or Vulnerability in Urban Development', *Regional Development Dialogue*, 5:2, pp. 135-170.

Munro, I. (1987), speech given at the Second International Shelter Conference, and published in *Proceedings of the Second International Shelter Conference and Vienna Recommendations on Shelter and Urban Development*, National Association of Realtors, Washington, p. 105.

Neocosmos, M. (1986), 'Marx's Third Class: Capitalist Landed Property and Capitalist Development', *Journal of Peasant Studies*, 13:3, pp. 5-44.

Nun, J.; Alvarez, A.; Sandoval, E. and Arroyo, R. (1978), *A situação da classe trabalhadora na América Latina*, Centro de Estudos de Cultura Contemporanea, São Paulo.

Ofori, G. (1980), 'The Construction Industries of Developing Countries: The Applicability of Existing Theories and Strategies for Their Improvement and Lessons for the Future - the Case of Ghana', Ph.D. dissertation, University College London.

Ofori, G. (1989), 'Housing in Ghana: The Case for a Central Executive Agency', *Habitat International*, 13:1, pp. 5-18.

Oliveira, F. (1972), *A Economia Brasileira: crítica à razão dualista*, Estudos CEBRAP 2, São Paulo.

Ozuekren, S. (1989), 'Employment Practices in Housing Construction in Turkey', *Trialog*, 1-II:20, pp. 30-35.

PADCO/USAID (Planning and Development Collaborative International/Office of Housing and Urban Programs, United States Agency for International Development) (1985), 'Peru Shelter Sector Assessment Volume II', Technical Report, USAID, Washington, July.

Pfeifer, U. (1987), 'A West German Perspective', *Proceedings of the Second International Shelter Conference and Vienna Recommendations on Shelter and Urban Development*, National Association of Realtors, Washington, pp. 86-88.

Phillip, M. (1987), 'Urban Low-Income Housing in St. Lucia: An Analysis of the Formal and Informal Sectors', M.Phil. dissertation, University College London.

Piore, M. and Sabel, C. (1984), *The Second Industrial Divide: Possibilities for Prosperity*, Basic Books, New York.

Pradilla, E. (1976), 'Notas acerca del 'problema de la vivienda", *Ideologia y Sociedad*, 16, pp. 70-107.

Prandi, J. (1978), *O Trabalhador por Conta Própria sob o Capital*, Símbolo, São Paulo.

Preparatory Group Participants of the Vienna Recommendations on Shelter and Urban Development (1987), 'The Vienna Recommendations on Shelter and Urban Development', *Proceedings of the Second International Shelter Conference and Vienna Recommendations on Shelter and Urban Development*, National Association of Realtors, Washington, pp. 93-103.

Quijano, A. (1974), 'The Marginal Pole of the Economy and the Marginalized Labour Force', *Economy and Society*, 3:4, pp. 393-428.; and later published in Wolpe, H. (ed.) (1980), *The Articulation of Modes of Production*, Routledge & Kegan Paul, London, pp. 254-288.

Rakodi, C. (1989), 'The Production of Housing in Harare, Zimbabwe: Components, Constraints and Policy Outcomes', *Trialog*, 1-II:20, pp. 7-13.

Rakodi, C. (1991), 'Developing institutional capacity to meet the housing needs of the urban poor - experience in Kenya, Tanzania and Zambia', *Cities*, 8:3, pp. 228-243.

Ramachandran, A. (1987), 'The Worldwide Shelter Condition Today', *Proceedings of the Second International Shelter Conference and Vienna Recommendations on Shelter and Urban Development*, National Association of Realtors, Washington, pp. 45-49.

Ramachandran, A. (1990), 'A Global Strategy for Shelter: Dream or Reality?', address given at the Third International Shelter Conference, and quoted in Boleat, M. (1990), 'Third International Shelter Conference', *Housing Finance International*, August, p. 4.

Rasmussen, J. (1990), 'Small Urban Centres and the Development of Local Enterprises in Zimbabwe', in Baker, J. (ed.), *Small Town Africa*, Seminar Proceedings 23, Scandinavian Institute of African Studies, Uppsala.

Renaud, B. (1987), 'Resource Mobilization, Household Savings and Housing: The Emerging Agenda', *Proceedings of the Second International Shelter Conference and Vienna Recommendations on Shelter and Urban Development*, National Association of Realtors, Washington, pp. 60-66.

Richwine, A. (1987), 'Potential Areas for Intervention within the Informal Housing Sector', Background Paper, Informal Sector Strategy Development, Office of Housing and Urban Programs, United States Agency for International Development.

Rodwin, L. and Sanyal, B. (1987), 'Shelter, settlement and development: An Overview', in Rodwin, L. (ed.), *Shelter, Settlement and Development*, Allen & Unwin, Boston, pp. 3-31.

Rudra, A. (1988), 'Pre-Capitalist Modes of Production in Non-European Societies', *Journal of Peasant Studies*, 15:3, pp. 373-394.

Saini, B. (1985), 'Barefoot Architects: A Training Program for Building in the Third World', in Lea, J. and Courtney, J. (eds), *Cities in Conflict - Studies in the Planning and Management of Asian Cities*, a World Bank Symposium, The World Bank, Washington.

Santos, M. (1979), *The Shared Space - The Two Circuits of the Urban Economy in Underdeveloped Countries*, Methuen, London.

Sayer, A. (1988), 'Post Fordism in Question', *Society and Space - Environment and Planning D*, 9:3, pp. 321-336.

Schmitz, H. (1982), *Manufacturing in the Backyard - Case Studies on Accumulation and Employment in Small-scale Brazilian Industry*, Frances Pinter, London.

Schmitz, H. (1989), 'Flexible Specialisation - A New Paradigm of Small-Scale Industrialisation?' Discussion Paper of the Institute of Development Studies 261, University of Sussex.

Schonberger, G. (1988), 'From Fordism to flexible accumulation: technology, competitive strategies, and international location', *Society and Space - Environment and Planning D*, 6:3, pp. 245-262.

Schumacher, E. (1973), *Small is Beautiful - A Study of Economics as If People Mattered*, Blond & Briggs, London.

Scott, A. (1979), 'Who are the Self-Employed?' in Bromley, R. and Gerry, C. (eds), *Casual Work and Poverty in Third World Cities*, John Wiley & Sons, Chichester, pp. 105-129.

Scott, A. (1986a), 'Introduction: Why Rethink Petty Commodity Production?', in Scott, A. (ed.), 'Rethinking Petty-Commodity Production', *Social Analysis*, Special Issue Series, 20, pp. 3-10.

Scott, A. (1986b), 'Towards a Rethinking of Petty Commodity Production', in Scott, A. (ed.), 'Rethinking Petty-Commodity Production', *Social Analysis*, Special Issue Series, 20, pp. 93-105.

Smith, C. (1986), 'Reconstructing the Elements of Petty Commodity Production', in Scott, A (ed.), 'Rethinking Petty-Commodity Production', *Social Analysis*, Special Issue Series, 20, pp. 29-46.

Stimpson, J. (1987), 'North American Shelter Systems: Lessons for Developing Countries - The United States Experience', *Proceedings of the Second International Shelter Conference and Vienna Recommendations on Shelter and Urban Development*, National Association of Realtors, Washington, pp. 80-82.

Strassman, W. (1988), 'Small-Scale Construction Methods, Building Materials, and Home-Based Enterprises in the Informal Sector', Discussion Paper for a Workshop on the Role of the Informal Sector in Providing Housing and Infrastructure in Developing Countries, sponsored by the Office of Housing and Urban Programs, United States Agency for International Development.

Stretton, A. (1978), 'Independent Foremen and the Construction of Formal Sector Housing in the Greater Manila Area', in Rimmer, P.; Drakakis-Smith, D. and McGee T. (eds), *Food, Shelter and Transportation in the Southeast Asia and the Pacific*, Research School of Pacific Studies, Department of Human Geography, Publication HG/12, The Australian National University, Canberra, pp. 155-170.

Taschner, S. and Mautner, Y. (1982), 'Habitação da Pobreza: Alternativas de Moradia Popular em São Paulo', Cadernos de Estudos e Pesquisas 5, Universidade de São Paulo.

Taylor, J. (1979), *From Modernization to Modes of Production*, Macmillan, London.

Terray, E. (1972), *Marxism and 'Primitive Societies'*, Monthly Review Press, New York.

Tuckman, A. (1983), 'Labour, Subcontracting and Capital Accumulation in the British Construction Industry', *The Production of the Built Environment - Proceedings of the 4th. Bartlett International Summer School*, Bartlett School of Architecture and Planning, London, pp. 1-10/1-22.

Tuffs, R. (1987), 'The Dual-Sector Concept: An Examination of Low-Cost Housing and Building in Penang, West Malaysia', M.A. dissertation, University of Keele.

Turin, D. (1973), 'Construction and Development', Building Economics Research Unit, University College London, mimeo; later published in *Habitat International* (1978), 3:1/2, pp. 33-45.

Turner, J. (1985), 'Practice for the 'Habitat Worker' and of 'Habitat Work"', in Oberlander, P. (ed.), *Habitat Worker: Training for Community Based Human Settlement Improvement*, University of British Columbia Centre for Human Settlements, Vancouver.

Turner, J. (1988a), 'Introduction', in Turner, B. (ed.), *Building Community - A Third World Case Book*, Building Community Books, London, pp. 13-18.

Turner, J. (1988b), 'Issues and Conclusions', in Turner, B. (ed.), *Building Community - A Third World Case Book*, Building Community Books, London, pp. 169-181

Turner, J. and Fitcher, R. (eds) (1972), *Freedom to Build: dweller control and the housing process*, Macmillan, New York.

UNCHS (United Nations Centre for Human Settlements) (1981), *Review of the Role and Contribution of the Construction Industry in Human Settlement Programmes and National Economic and Social Development*, UNCHS, Nairobi.

Urban Edge (1987), 'Making Housing Markets more Efficient', *Urban Edge*, 11:9, pp. 1-5.

Vargas, N. (1979), 'Organização do Trabalho e Capital - Um Estudo da Construção Habitacional', M.Sc. dissertation, Universidade Federal do Rio de Janeiro.

Vercruijsse, E. (1984), *The Penetration of Capitalism*, Zed Books, London.

Ward, P. (1982), 'Introduction and Purpose', in Ward, P., (ed.), *Self-Help Housing - A Critique*, Mansell, London, pp. 1-13.

Weeks, J. (1973), 'Uneven Sectoral Development and the Role of the State', *Bulletin of the Institute of Development Studies*, University of Sussex, 5:2/3, pp. 76-82.

Werna, E. (1994), 'The Provision of Low-cost Housing in Developing Countries: a Post- or a Pre-fordist Process of Production?', *Habitat International*, 18:3, pp. 95-103.

Widiono, M. (1989), 'The Investigation on the Aspect of Appropriate Construction Technology for the Provision of Shelter in Developing Countries', M.Sc. dissertation, University College London.

Wolpe, H. (1980), 'Introduction', in Wolpe, H. (ed.), *The Articulation of Modes of Production*, Routledge & Kegan Paul, London, pp. 1-43.

Wycliffe, R. (1987), 'Housing for the Low-Income Urban Population in Malawi: Towards an Alternative Approach', Ph.D. dissertation, University of Essex.

Index